FIRST
PEOPLES
of NORTH
AMERICA

THE PEOPLE AND CULTURE OF THE
CHEYENNE

CASSIE M. LAWTON
RAYMOND BIAL

Cavendish
Square
New York

Published in 2017 by Cavendish Square Publishing, LLC
243 5th Avenue, Suite 136, New York, NY 10016

Copyright © 2017 by Cavendish Square Publishing, LLC

First Edition

Website: cavendishsq.com

This publication represents the opinions and views of the author based on his or her personal experience, knowledge, and research. The information in this book serves as a general guide only. The author and publisher have used their best efforts in preparing this book and disclaim liability rising directly or indirectly from the use and application of this book.

CPSIA Compliance Information: Batch #CS16CSQ

All websites were available and accurate when this book was sent to press.

Library of Congress Cataloging-in-Publication Data

Names: Lawton, Cassie M., author. | Bial, Raymond, author. Title: The people and culture of the Cheyenne / Cassie M. Lawton and Raymond Bial. Description: New York : Cavendish Square Publishing, 2017. | Series: First peoples of North America | Includes bibliographical references and index. | Description based on print version record and CIP data provided by publisher; resource not viewed. Identifiers: LCCN 2015045092 (print) | LCCN 2015042981 (ebook) | ISBN 9781502618894 (ebook) | ISBN 9781502618887 (library bound) Subjects: LCSH: Cheyenne Indians--History--Juvenile literature. | Cheyenne Indians--Social life and customs--Juvenile literature. Classification: LCC E99.C53 (print) | LCC E99.C53 L39 2016 (ebook) | DDC 978.004/97353--dc23 LC record available at http://lccn.loc.gov/2015045092

Editorial Director: David McNamara
Editor: Kristen Susienka
Copy Editor: Rebecca Rohan
Art Director: Jeffrey Talbot
Designer: Amy Greenan
Production Assistant: Karol Szymczuk
Photo Research: J8 Media

Printed in the United States of America

ACKNOWLEDGMENTS

We would like to thank all of those individuals involved in this project, for their insight and their expertise. Especially, we would like to thank Cavendish Square for the publication of this book. As always, we offer deep appreciation for our families and friends for their support along the journey.

CONTENTS

AUTHORS' NOTE

At the dawn of the twentieth century, Native Americans were thought to be a vanishing race. However, despite four hundred years of warfare, deprivation, and disease, Native Americans have persevered. Countless thousands have lost their lives, but over the course of this century and the last, the populations of Native tribes have grown tremendously. Even as America's First Peoples struggle to adapt to modern Western life, they have also kept the flame of their traditions alive—the languages, religions, stories, and the everyday ways of life. An exhilarating renaissance in Native American culture is now sweeping the continent from coast to coast.

The First Peoples of North America books depict the social and cultural life of the major nations, from the early history of Native peoples in North America to their present-day struggles for survival and dignity. Historical and contemporary photographs of traditional subjects, as well as period illustrations, are blended throughout each book so that readers may gain a sense of family life in a tipi, a hogan, or a longhouse.

No single book can comprehensively portray the intricate and varied lifeways of an entire tribe, or nation. We only hope that young people will come away with a deeper appreciation for the rich tapestry of Native American culture—both then and now—and a keen desire to learn more about these first Americans.

Cheyenne warriors return to their tribe, circa 1910.

CHAPTER ONE

The stones are all that last long.

—Cheyenne war song

A CULTURE BEGINS

Since prehistoric times, people have populated North America. Most historians and archeologists agree that around ten thousand years ago, humans entered North America via the **Bering Strait**, a narrow land bridge that once connected Asia and Alaska. The first humans hunted for their food and collected nuts, berries, or other vegetation for protein and **sustenance**. As humans evolved, they became more unified. They gathered in family groups and later settled into villages. Some Native people traveled together across the land, following herds of bison or other large animals, while others, over time, stayed in one region and built permanent communities. Among these first people were the ancestors of many present-day Native American tribes, including the Cheyenne.

The First Cheyenne

A **nomadic** people, the Cheyenne originally lived in the north-central part of the present-day United States or the south-central region of present-day Canada, near the source of the Mississippi River, probably along the southern shores of the Great Lakes. They may also have spread as far as the northern shore and western end of Lake Superior. Before 1700, they lived mainly in Minnesota. Eventually, circumstances led many to relocate farther west, into North and South Dakota, Colorado, Wyoming, and Montana.

The first Cheyenne people called themselves the Tsistsistas (tsiss-TSISS-tahss), meaning "our people." They spoke Algonquian, a type of language shared with other Native American tribes, including the Arapaho, the Delaware, and the Shawnee. The name Cheyenne may come from a Sioux word *Shai-ela*, referring to "people who speak a strange language."

For many years, the Cheyenne practiced an agrarian lifestyle. The women tended the crops while the men stalked deer, rabbits, and other small animals in the woods and caught fish in the clear, rushing streams.

When game became scarce, they moved to other parts of the northern forests, relying on dogs to pull their **travois** (trav-OY), small sleds on which they loaded their belongings. The dogs also carried bundles strapped on their backs.

Before their westward migration, the woods, wildlife, and waters of Minnesota provided the Cheyenne with food, clothing, and shelter. There were animals to eat and rivers in which to bathe or from which to drink. Over the years, illnesses and aggression from neighboring tribes made it more difficult for the Cheyenne to live in their chosen area. By the late 1600s, several tribes had moved across the Mississippi River and onto the **Great Plains**.

Entering the Great Plains

For nearly a century, the Cheyenne wandered over vast stretches of prairie—rolling grasslands that flow wave upon wave as far as the eye can see. Occasionally, the sweep of land was broken by a streambed, along with a ragged line of trees whose leaves rustled in the wind. Much of the landscape was rippled with hills and ridges, as well as small mountains or buttes that rose abruptly. Often, far into the distance, there was a jagged row of white-capped mountains. In other places, the land was so flat that it appeared to be the floor of the sky.

This vast, open country, with the sky towering overhead, gave the Cheyenne a sense of utter freedom. Spreading far and wide, the plains were laced by several broad, often shallow rivers—the Missouri, the Platte, the North Platte, and the Cimarron. The riverbanks were fringed with cottonwood trees whose leaves turned

The Cheyenne lived on the Great Plains for centuries.

bright yellow in the autumn. The Cheyenne often camped near these rivers where the clear flowing waters cut shallow ravines in the otherwise unbroken land. However freeing, this land also offered hardships. Here, the Cheyenne had a little shelter from enemies and the weather, especially the unrelenting wind.

This region was noted for its extreme weather. There were hot, humid summers—especially on the southern plains—and winters were always brutal in the North Country. Fierce winds rushed down from the Arctic, along with heavy snows and bitter cold. One could easily get lost in a blizzard, blinded by the swirling wall of white, and quickly freeze to death. Yet the northern plains also had gentle seasons—the tender green of spring, the bloom of summer, and the golden light of autumn. But much of this precious time of warmth was devoted to getting ready for the next blasts of winter.

Amid the sweet grasses, the prairie was fragrant with the scent of sage and other herbs used by medicine

The People and Culture of the Cheyenne

men in healing rituals. Within the broad prairies were two extraordinary landscapes in South Dakota, one haunted—the Badlands—and the other holy—the Black Hills—near which the Cheyenne settled for a time. The Badlands was a place of fantastic, contorted rock sculptures. The land was mostly colorless, so the pale gray rock formations resembled the surface of the moon. It was a strange, mystical place, strewn with the fossilized bones of dinosaurs and other ancient creatures. The Plains people, including the Cheyenne, believed it was haunted. Ghosts, monsters, and evil spirits wandered the land, and the Cheyenne avoided the Badlands. Rising suddenly from the prairie, cool and full of mysterious shadows, were the Black Hills. In this high country, the treeless prairie gave way to meadows enclosed by rocky hills spiked with dark pine trees. There were also clear lakes surrounded by spruce and ponderosa pine trees, as well as juniper and quaking aspens. The Black Hills included many rocky outcroppings, including the Needles and the Cathedral Spires, which reached upward in this holy place. This was a sacred region to the Cheyenne and the Sioux, who were good friends and strong allies.

Many animals also made their homes on the prairies and forests of Cheyenne country. The most prominent was the bison, also called buffalo. In the 1500s, it is estimated there were more than sixty million living on the plains. Beneath the sea of bison there were whole towns of prairie dogs, the rodents popping up, then diving back down into their burrows. There were swift, graceful pronghorn antelope springing away like sudden gusts of wind. Wild horses also came to run free across the plains. Over time, the Cheyenne would rely on horses for transportation in everyday life and on the battlefield. Birds tended nests carefully hidden on the ground, and the roving coyote trotted along, always looking for a meal. Overhead circled vultures, hawks, and eagles. Falcons swooped down upon mourning doves, while sandhill cranes waded through the shallow water along the edges of streams.

Rivers threading through the North Country teemed with fish, including carp, sturgeon, and yellow bullhead. From mid-May through June, ancient paddlefish ran in the murky waters of the Yellowstone River, while trout zipped through the nearby Bighorn River. Up in the surrounding hills, elk, moose, bighorn sheep, and mule deer nibbled grass, always keeping alert for bobcats, mountain lions, wolves, black bears, and grizzlies. Wild turkeys, partridge, and grouse also fed among the trees.

Occasionally, the Cheyenne killed a bison. When the Cheyenne first encountered the Europeans in the 1680s, the shaggy beasts ranged as far east as the Appalachian Mountains. The Cheyenne came to realize that the bison could provide nearly all their basic needs—food, clothing, and shelter. Seeing the enormous bison herds that roamed the grasslands, they migrated across the Mississippi River in a westerly direction to the Great Plains of present-day South Dakota. There they lived from around 1700 to 1780. Other tribes eventually drove the Cheyenne southwest to the Black Hills of present-day South Dakota, near the headwaters of the Cheyenne River. The Lewis and Clark expedition of the early 1800s found them living there in 1804. Numbering more than 3,500 people, the Cheyenne were made up of at least

For centuries, millions of bison roamed the grasslands of the plains.

twenty bands, including the Suhtai, a tribe that had been absorbed into the Cheyenne in the early 1800s. Around 1806, they moved southwest to present-day Wyoming and then almost due south to Colorado.

The Significance of Horses

Before the Spanish brought horses to North America in the 1500s, Cheyenne life was very difficult. They were restricted in their travels to the small loads a dog or person could drag on a travois. When the first horse arrived in Cheyenne territory in the 1700s, their way of life changed dramatically. Now that they could haul heavier loads, the Cheyenne made larger houses, called **tipis** (TEE-peez), and traveled greater distances between their summer and winter camps. As the Cheyenne became skilled riders, they could hunt the thundering herds of bison and wage war over even broader stretches of land. A man's wealth came to be counted in the number of horses he owned. By the early 1800s, as the Cheyenne moved onto the open prairies, they completely abandoned their permanent villages and followed the herds on their swift horses. As they came in contact with the Sioux and other plains tribes, they gradually adopted many of their customs, styles of dress, and daily habits. They also began to practice a sacred religious rite known as the **Sun Dance**, which they adopted from the Sioux.

The Cheyenne and Europeans

For centuries, the Cheyenne were one of the dominant tribes of the Great Plains. However, their world would change with the arrival of European explorers, traders, and settlers.

Europeans first recorded contact with the Cheyenne in 1680, when a group of the Natives visited a French fort on the Illinois River and invited the French to come to their territory on the upper Mississippi, where there was abundant wildlife. Later, in their homes on the plains of Montana, South Dakota, Wyoming, and Colorado, they would again face settlers. This time, the Europeans would completely change the Cheyenne's way of life by forcing them from their land and impressing on them European lifestyles, customs, and beliefs.

Originally, Western traders introduced iron kettles, cloth, and guns to the Cheyenne. The guns helped in hunting but also intensified warfare among the tribes. Battles had previously been marked by bravery,

Little Robe, a Cheyenne member, poses for a photo, circa 1920.

skill, and daring as warriors **counted coup**, which involved getting close enough to an enemy to touch him. But guns changed the ways of warfare. Warriors could now shoot their enemies from a distance. The Cheyenne fiercely battled other tribes, especially the Crow and Kiowa, yet allied themselves with the powerful Sioux, as they established themselves on the Great Plains.

In 1825, on the Teton River in the Rocky Mountains, the Cheyenne signed their first **treaty** with the United States. The government promised to protect the Cheyenne in exchange for permission to build Bent's Fort in their hunting territory on the upper Arkansas River in Colorado. After the fort was built, the tribe split into two groups: the Southern Cheyenne, who moved to the Arkansas River, and the Northern Cheyenne, who ranged around the headwaters of the Platte and Yellowstone Rivers. The tribes were formally separated by the Treaty of Fort Laramie in 1851.

Over the course of the century, the Southern Cheyenne bands moved farther west to the upper branches of the Platte River, driving their rivals, the Kiowa, to the south. In 1840, they made peace with the Kiowa after a battle along Wolf Creek in what is now northwestern Oklahoma. Over time, they also became allies with the Comanche, Arapaho, Kiowa, and Kiowa-Apache. Yet, for nearly a century, they terrified their enemies as they galloped across the prairie, feathers streaming from their hair and war paint streaking their faces. With their quick horses, they were able to hunt enough buffalo in a single day to feed their people for months, leaving the young men free to race across the plains in war parties that ranged more than a thousand miles from Oklahoma to Montana.

Telling Stories

The Cheyenne passed the histories of their tribes and their beliefs down through many stories. These tales explained their origins, sacred rites, and the daring acts of their heroes, notably Motzeyoef (mott-zee-IH-oo-uf), or Sweet Medicine. Through storytelling, the Cheyenne ensured the survival of their customs and traditions.

Like other Plains tribes, the Cheyenne trace their origin to a time when the world was submerged by a great flood. As legend has it, floating on the water, a spiritual being convinced the waterfowl to dive beneath the surface and look for soil. The swans and geese failed to bring up soil, but finally a little duck returned with mud in its bill. When this mud dried, the earth was created. The spiritual being then shaped some of the soft ground into a man and a woman. Symbolizing summer and winter, the man and the woman caused the changes in seasons and weather. However, they could not have children, so the spiritual being made other people who could multiply and populate the earth.

It is said that the first Cheyenne lived underground. They were led to the surface by one of their more daring leaders, who was himself guided by a small light to the world above. Other stories have to do with survival and especially with the search for food. Here is the story of how the Cheyenne's two most important foods, corn and buffalo, were brought to them:

The People and Culture of the Cheyenne

When the Cheyenne still lived in the North, they made a camp in the form of a circle. At the entrance was a spring from which clear water tumbled down the hillside. Although they had plenty of fresh water, the people had little food and were very hungry. One day, the men were playing a game with a hoop and sticks. A large crowd gathered to watch the contest, including a young man from the south side of the camp. His body was painted yellow, and in his hair he wore a yellow eagle feather. He was wrapped in a buffalo robe.

Soon another young man came from the north side of the camp circle. He was dressed exactly like the first. The two young men were surprised that they were dressed alike. The contestants paused in their game as the two men angrily confronted each other.

"Why are you copying me?" demanded the man from the south side.

The man from the north side asked if the other were trying to mock him.

They told each other that they had waded in the spring where an old woman had told them to dress this way. But they did not know why the old woman had asked them to do so. The young men declared that they would search for her at the spring. Everyone watched as they approached the water. Pulling their buffalo robes over their heads, they disappeared behind the curtain of water and found themselves in a large cave.

Sitting near the entrance, the old woman was cooking buffalo meat and corn in clay pots. She said to them, "Grandchildren, I have been expecting you. I am cooking for you. Please sit down beside me."

The young men sat down on either side of her. They told her that their people were starving.

She gave them corn from one pot and buffalo meat from the other. The young men ate their fill, but when they were done, their pots remained full.

The old woman told the young men to look toward the south. There they saw grasslands covered with buffalo. She told them to gaze to the west, and they saw animals of all shapes and sizes, including horses, which the Cheyenne had never seen before. She told them to look north, and they saw corn growing lush and tall.

Then the old woman said to them, "When you leave this place, the buffalo will follow you. Your people will see them before sunset. Carry this uncooked corn in your robes. Every spring, plant the seeds in low, moist ground. When the corn ripens, you will have enough food for your entire nation. Also take the cooked meat and corn and ask your people to sit down and eat in this order: males oldest to youngest, except for one orphan boy, then all females from oldest to youngest, except one orphan girl. After everyone has eaten, the two orphans may have what is left in the pots."

The two young men followed the old woman's instructions. As they passed through the water again, their entire bodies turned red, even the feathers on their heads.

The people ate from the pots, which remained full until the orphan boy and girl ate all the remaining food. As sunset approached, the people returned to the spring to find buffalo leaping out of the water. One after another, buffalo emerged from the spring all through the night and the following day until a vast herd stretched across the plains.

The Cheyenne surrounded the herd of buffalo. Though on foot, the men ran very fast as they hunted, soon killing many buffalo and bringing back plenty of meat. Moving their camp to low, marshy ground, they planted the corn the old woman had given the young men. Every one of the seeds sprouted and grew into tall, leafy stalks, each of which bore two or more ears of corn. Every year thereafter, the Cheyenne planted corn and hunted buffalo, and they never went hungry again.

The Cheyenne were central to the plains for centuries, until settlers wanted their land and pushed them out.

Cheyenne chief
Two Moons.

CHAPTER TWO

Our first teacher is our own heart.

—Cheyenne saying

BUILDING A CIVILIZATION

Over time, the Cheyenne community developed into a thriving civilization. They had their own government, warriors, beliefs, language, and traditions. They believed that everything in nature had a place and should be respected. When the Europeans arrived, many could not understand the Cheyenne's lifestyle and sought to change their view of the world. The Cheyenne, despite these hardships, continued as one of the main tribes in the region, challenging the various governments that wanted to change them.

The Seasons and Community Life

The Cheyenne lived in harmony with the cycle of the twelve months, marked by the passage of the moons, each of which had a name. There was the Hoop Moon (January), the Big Hoop Moon (February), the Powder-Faced Moon (March), the Hollow Tree Moon (April), the New Growth Moon (May), the Planting Moon (June), the Giving Moon (July), the Harvest Moon (August), the Cold-Faced Moon (September), the Icy-Faced Moon (October), the Hard-Faced Moon (November), and the Big Hard-Faced Moon (December). According to each moon, the Cheyenne concentrated on an activity, such as hunting or harvesting, or the weather to be faced. During the winters, they camped on the low embankments of rivers, away from the blowing snow. As spring approached, the men hunted deer, elk, bears, and pronghorns, as well as wild turkeys, prairie chickens, and rabbits. The women gathered the first of the wild berries and fruit. Before going onto the plains to hunt, they let the buffalo fatten on the tender sprigs of April grass.

The Cheyenne lived in bands, or groups, of family members. Each band had one or more chiefs, generally older men chosen for their wealth and wisdom. A leader also had to be courageous and clever, or another warrior would replace him. In addition to maintaining order in the village, the chiefs decided when the band would move, when they would embark on a bison hunt, and where they would make their next camp. Leaders usually conferred with medicine men to determine the best time to hunt. Then scouts were dispatched to find the bison herds.

Chief Dull Knife became an important figure for the Cheyenne people.

Along with the chiefs and other respected leaders, young men who had proven themselves in combat could lead war parties. No one was forced to join a war party, but if a certain leader had been successful, other warriors were generally eager to ride with him. However, none of the leaders had great influence, even within the band. Living in small groups, the Cheyenne did not need a complicated system for governing themselves. They relied primarily on ridicule and gossip to punish anyone who broke the rules. Sometimes, a council of older men gathered to help resolve a dispute, but they lacked the authority to enforce any decision. It was a man's prowess as a hunter and warrior and a woman's ability in providing for her family that mattered most to the members of the band. Strength and skill were essential for survival on the open plains—although generosity was also admired. A wealthy man with many horses enjoyed prestige and was expected to share his food and belongings with others in events called "giveaways."

Cheyenne families included children, parents, grandparents, and unmarried aunts and uncles. Grandmothers often helped with chores around the tipi and looked after the young children. Although men headed the household, children traced their family heritage through both parents. Bands were bound together by the male relatives—fathers, sons, and brothers. When a young man married, he usually remained with his father's band. The Cheyenne believed that men who had grown up together worked better as a group. Mutual respect, cooperation, and understanding ensured safety and success in the dangerous tasks of hunting and warfare. Even small raids to steal horses usually included several closely related men.

The Cheyenne loved to get together with others, and a buffalo stew or other tasty meal was always simmering over the fire. Gathering in the tipi, people played games, told stories, or boasted of their mighty deeds of skill and courage. Boasting was encouraged because warriors had to be strong and brave to hunt bison, defeat their enemies, and endure the cold winters. Men loved to gamble and seldom engaged in a contest that didn't involve a bet. Guessing games, such as the **Moccasin** Game, were also enjoyed. The Moccasin Game involved three soft leather shoes with a small rock placed under one of them. Adults bet on which moccasin was hiding the pebble. Visits usually ended with a pipe smoking. As the aroma of red willow bark and tobacco wafted through the night air, the pipe was reverently handed from one man to another.

This image shows Southern Cheyenne housing, circa 1900.

Dwellings

When the Cheyenne made their home in the Dakotas, they lived in earthen lodges of wooden frames covered with sod. At this time, they farmed patches of land in addition to hunting and gathering, and they did not need to move very often. However, as they began to hunt and rely on bison, they adopted the tipi, which was better suited to their new, nomadic way of life. The tipi was the Cheyenne's standard dwelling for families and large groups of people living on the plains. It was constructed from animal hides and poles and usually assumed a triangular shape. Some tipis were large, able to hold an entire village, while others were small, more suited for housing a family. A horse pulling a travois could easily transport a tipi. The Cheyenne often decorated their tipis with painted designs they had received during visions.

Good manners governed life in the tipi. When people gathered around the fire for meals and conversation, the men always sat on buffalo rugs on the north side. Women sat on the south. The head of the household always held the place of honor within the circle at the back of the tipi, along with his willow backrest, pipe rack, and sacred things. It was considered impolite to walk between a person and the fire. Men, especially visitors, were always served meals first. Women and children had to wait until the warriors were done eating.

To make tipis, men went into the hills to chop down long, slender pine trees for the framework. The strong, light trunks were dried in the sun, then dragged back to the camp. Women lashed three of the poles together and raised them. Spreading out the bottom ends of the poles, they stood the frame upright. Then they placed about twenty poles in the gaps to complete the cone-shaped frame. At one time, the Cheyenne covered their lodges with sheets of bark, but after moving onto the plains they began to use bison hides.

To make the covering, women first spread fresh hides on the ground and scraped away the fat and flesh with bone or antler blades. They dried the hides in the sun and scraped off the coarse brown hair. After soaking the hides in water for a few days, they laboriously rubbed in a mixture of animal fat, brains, and liver to soften the hides. They rinsed the hides in water and repeatedly worked them back and forth over a rawhide rope to

The Cheyenne made their structures using wooden poles.

soften them further. Finally, the hides were smoked over a fire to give them a pleasing tan color.

To complete the cover, several women laid out about fifteen tanned hides and carefully stitched them together. The covering was attached to a pole and raised, then wrapped around the frame. Held together with wooden pins, the covering had two wing-shaped flaps turned back at the top to form a smoke hole. The flaps could be closed to keep out the rain, as could the hide flap covering the oval-shaped doorway. Always facing east toward the rising sun, the doorway was often adorned with strips of rawhide, porcupine quills, feathers, or horsetails.

During a summer heat wave, the bottom edges of the tipi could be raised to allow the wind to blow through. During the winter, people often banked the tipi with a berm, or sloped earthen wall, for better insulation. They also hung a dew cloth made of bison hides on the inside walls from about shoulder-height down to the damp ground. Decorated with paintings of battles, dreams, and visions, the dew cloth kept out dampness and created pockets of insulating air. With a fire burning in the center of the earthen floor and animal hides lining the walls, tipis stayed warm throughout the coldest winter months.

The tipi made an excellent home for the nomadic Cheyenne. Working together, several women could easily set it up or take it down in a few minutes. Then they used the tipi poles as a travois to carry the bulky covering and their belongings to the next camp. The poles were strapped to a horse's shoulders so they dragged on the ground behind it. This proved to work

The People and Culture of the Cheyenne

even better than wheels on the bumpy ground of the prairie and hills.

They also built dome-shaped buildings called **sweat lodges**. These dwellings were very important to the Cheyenne and continue to hold significance today. The Cheyenne's religious ceremonies take place inside these sweat lodges, as ancestors of the present-day Cheyenne were once taught by the holy man known as Sweet Medicine. Ceremonies, called sweats, are carried out throughout the year. The Cheyenne today consider their sweat lodges to be places of ultimate spirituality.

With the introduction of horses, Cheyenne warriors could travel faster.

Life on the Plains

Originally, the Cheyenne had only half-wild dogs as working animals. However, that changed in the late 1700s when the Cheyenne encountered wild horses on the plains. The great prophet Sweet Medicine predicted

A Cheyenne gathering.

the horse's coming: "Those far hills that seem only a blue vision in the distance take many days to reach now, but with this animal you can get there in a short time, so fear him not." By the 1800s, herds of wild horses ranged throughout the American West. The Cheyenne came to rely heavily on these animals that enabled them to travel faster and farther. Men captured and broke, or tamed, wild mustangs but preferred to trade or steal horses that had already been broken. Stealing horses from a rival tribe became a daring art among the Plains tribes. A successful raid brought prestige and battle honors, and the size of one's herd became a symbol of wealth. Horses became a primary means of exchange, and giving horses away was highly respected.

The People and Culture of the Cheyenne

Constantly on the move, the Cheyenne no longer planted corn or hunted small game. Why toil in the fields or stalk game in the woods when men could leap onto their horses and race after the buffalo herds? In a single hunt, they could obtain enough meat to feed the band for months, as well as a wealth of hides and bones for fashioning tipis and tools. Their nomadic way of life required that household goods be light and durable and easily carried to the next camp. Thus pottery—the art form they had practiced for decades—was impractical because it could be broken on their long journeys. Instead, they stored food, clothing, and other personal belongings in leather pouches called parfleches (par-FLESH-es). They carried water in animal skins and cooked meat and vegetables in the lining of a buffalo stomach.

If the herds continued to graze in the vicinity, the band might remain there for several weeks or months. But more often, bands had to stay in pursuit of the herds. Usually, the Cheyenne made camp near streams and woods, where they had a ready supply of freshwater for cooking and drinking and plenty of wood for their fires. Often at war with the other Plains tribes, especially the Crow, the Cheyenne picked campsites that could be easily defended against attack and often returned to their favorite camping places year after year.

Over the years, the Cheyenne adapted to and thrived in life on the plains. They set up communities and traveled from region to region, following the bison's migration patterns. In the 1800s, however, the first settlers arrived, challenging the Cheyenne's very existence.

A young Cheyenne child in a cradleboard.

*Great Spirit, bless
our children, friends,
and visitors through
a happy life. May our
trails lie straight and
level before us.*

—Plains People prayer

LIFE IN THE CHEYENNE TRIBES

Prior to the arrival of Europeans, the Cheyenne's way of life was familiar. Daily life followed a routine. The customs of life and death became part of the Cheyenne's beliefs. Many children knew they were cherished by their relatives and encouraged to follow the beliefs and traditions of their people. No matter the hardships they faced, the Cheyenne were unified in their care for one another and for the land.

The Life Cycle

For the Cheyenne, certain traditions accompanied the cycle of life and death. There were different customs for each stage of life. Eventually, the children of the tribe would grow into men and women capable of leading it into the future and preserving the history of their ancestors from generation to generation.

Being Born

The birth of a child was a joyous occasion. When a woman was about to go into labor, one or more older women served as her midwives inside the tipi. Men were not allowed in the tipi while she was giving birth.

As soon as the baby was born, it was snugly wrapped and protected from the weather. If the baby was born during the cold and stormy weather, the mother held it close to her warm body for several months. Nonetheless, many infants born in the winter died from the frigid temperatures. During the warmer months, the mother secured her baby in a **cradleboard**. The infant spent most of the day in the cradleboard, which the mother hung on a lodge pole or leaned against the tipi. The baby could watch her as she cooked at the fire or tanned bison hides and worked about the camp. If the camp moved, the mother fastened the cradleboard to her saddle or travois pole. When the baby wasn't in the cradleboard, it was either crawling on the ground or wrapped in a blanket or robe and carried on its mother's back. The mother often played with her baby to keep it amused.

At three to six months of age, the baby had its ears pierced in a special ceremony. The father presented a gift of one to three horses to the person asked to do the piercing. As the child grew up, the father might have the youngster's ears pierced several times.

Occasionally, formal names were given to a child at the time of birth. A father might send for the newborn, gather it in his arms, and give the baby a name and a horse. He might declare, "I give him my name," or he might name the infant after a beloved relative. However, a small child often had only a pet name, such as "pot belly," meant as a term of endearment. By the time the child turned six or seven, however, he or she was named after a relative. Over the years, the child received other names based on character traits or noteworthy events.

Children in the Tribe

The Cheyenne looked upon their children as a wonderful gift. Children were never whipped and rarely punished. They were taught to be generous with others and respectful of elders. From an early age, children were treated as adults and permitted to make many of their own decisions. Parents encouraged boys to model themselves after the most skilled hunters and warriors. Similarly, girls were taught to look up to the women who were most diligent in caring for their families.

At an early age, boys were given small bows and arrows to practice shooting at birds. Playing with dolls and toy tipis, girls learned to care for families. As soon as they learned to walk, they followed their mothers, fetching wood and water. Eventually, they were taught how to cut moccasins and to do **quillwork**, as well as to dress bison hides.

The Cheyenne made intricate crafts and objects, such as this quilled horse mask.

Children were allowed to run free, and the entire outdoors became their playground. Both girls and boys learned to ride horses as soon as they learned to walk. Soon after he learned to ride, a boy helped out at his first buffalo hunt. He served as a water boy or fire keeper while he learned how the men hunted. Both girls and boys also played vigorous games of running, jumping, and fighting, as well as races on foot and on horseback. During the summer, they played in the streams and became excellent swimmers. Cheyenne children had to strengthen their bodies if they were going to survive the rugged life of hunters and warriors.

Despite the intense competition of their games, children got along very well. In fact, they were usually cheerful and cooperative with each other. Often, children had a play camp not far from their parents' tipis. The girls set up poles for tipis, took care of the children, and prepared meals. Riding sticks served as horses, and the boys pretended to hunt bison and go to war.

During the winter months, children gathered around their grandfathers and listened to stories about the creation of the Cheyenne and the great deeds of Sweet Medicine. Old men also spoke of their own heroism in battles and bison hunts. With no written language, children learned the history and customs of their people orally, in the hope that someday they, too, would pass on the traditions.

Growing Up

When he was about twelve years old, a young man was reminded of his duty to prove himself as a hunter and warrior. He needed to provide for his mother and family and protect the band, as well as conduct himself properly around the camp. At this age or a little older, he might join the men as a hunter. If he was lucky enough to kill a buffalo calf, his father held a feast in his honor and gave away one of his finest horses to another member of the band. The young man might also receive a new name to acknowledge his courageous deed. It was an important turning point in the boy's life. If he did well on the buffalo hunt, he would then be allowed to join a war party.

Grandfathers or older men often counseled the young man to avoid dangerous mistakes and to make wise decisions. If he killed a fat buffalo, he was advised to share the meat with an old, hungry man who could no longer hunt very well. The old man would then likely pray for the young man: "May you live to be as old as I am and always have good luck in your hunting. May you and your family live long and always have abundance."

As she matured, a young woman was carefully watched by her mother, aunts, and grandmothers. They advised her to stay at home and not wander about the camp. The young woman was told to leave the lodge only in the company of others. Her mother might say to her, "When you grow up to be a young woman, if you see someone you like, you must not be foolish and run off with him. You must marry properly. If you do so, you will become a good woman and will be a help to your brothers and your cousins."

At the onset of her first menstrual period, a girl told her mother who in turn informed her father. The father then declared the news from the doorway of the tipi and gave away a horse. The young woman unbraided her hair and bathed, after which older women painted her body red. With a robe drawn around her naked body, she sat near a hot coal drawn from the fire. Sweetgrass, juniper needles, and white sage were sprinkled over the coal, and the sacred smoke wafted over the young woman.

During this time, she had to observe a number of taboos. For four days, she could eat only roasted meat and was not allowed to ride a horse. She could not touch weapons or sacred objects. Young men could not eat or drink from a bowl she had used. Thereafter, during every period, she had to sleep in a special lodge in the camp and carefully follow these practices.

Marrying

Traditionally, if a man was fond of a young woman, he waited for her as she went for wood or water. If she would not stop to talk with him, the young man went away. As time went on, men adopted the Sioux practice of approaching the young woman's tipi with a blanket or robe over his head. He waited for her to come out, then threw the blanket around her and began to talk with her. If she did not like him, she broke away and he left humiliated. If she felt a spark of interest, they would talk for hours. To express a commitment to each other, they exchanged rings. Or he might take the bracelet from her wrist. She let him keep it if she wished to marry him.

If the young woman did not like her suitor, he might bring a pipe filled with tobacco to a medicine man who knew about love charms. Or he might ask the white-tailed deer for help. The deer was supposed to have great power in matters of the heart. The young man might carry love medicine in the tail of a deer and wear it on his shoulder belt.

White-tailed deer were important in matters of love for the Cheyenne.

Cheyenne women were honored for their chastity and often waited years before accepting a man in marriage. The man never proposed himself but asked a relative to bring gifts to the woman's family and ask on his behalf.

If the offer was accepted, the woman was brought to his tipi and carried inside on a blanket. She was dressed in new clothes, after which a great feast was held and gifts were exchanged between the families.

A man might have two or more wives. They often were the widows of slain warriors and frequently sisters. No matter the size of his family, a husband had to supply enough meat for everyone. The wives shared the chores but each had her own tipi for herself and her children.

Marriage was simply an agreement to live together. There were no spoken vows. Women were encouraged to marry and bear children. Virtue was expected of both the man and the woman. Divorces were possible if a couple didn't get along or if a spouse was unfaithful. To divorce, the wife simply placed her husband's belongings outside the tipi. A man would declare that he had "thrown his wife away" and not return home. For most couples, however, marriage was viewed as a lifetime commitment.

Dying

Whether a man died in battle or a woman of old age, the dying person was expected to face the moment with courage. Entering a time of deep mourning, the family prepared the body for its final resting place. The deceased was dressed in his or her finest clothing then wrapped in blankets or robes. People sang and prayed over the body. The bundle was carried from the tipi, lashed to a travois, and taken away. The Cheyenne feared ghosts, especially the ghosts of the dead who might snatch a living person away from the camp, so they held the funeral as soon as possible.

Overcome with grief, female relatives cut their hair. The wife, mother, and often the sisters slashed their legs. Sometimes, they chopped off a finger. Men did not cut themselves, but they did unbraid their hair.

A deceased warrior's gun, bow and arrows, knives, and tomahawk, along with his pipe and tobacco and other cherished personal belongings, were placed by his body. Offerings of food were sometimes tucked next to the body to comfort the soul. His finest horse was also killed so that its spirit might carry the dead warrior on his journey into the spirit world.

The body and possessions were placed in the branches of a tree or on a scaffold. Occasionally, the body was hidden in a cave or buried under a pile of rocks. It was believed that the spirit of the dead man found a trail on which the footprints all led in one direction—to the Milky Way. Following this path, the spirit arrived at the camp of the dead where it was reunited with friends and family members who had gone before.

War and War Societies

Trusted allies of the powerful Sioux, the Cheyenne were almost continually at war with the Crow, Pawnee, and Assiniboin who shared their hunting grounds. Warfare among the Plains tribes was a dangerous venture. Warriors could easily be killed, and despite the honor that came from heroic and daring acts, they valued their lives. Even in victory, a chief was shamed if he lost a single man from his party. For young warriors, the main reason for going into battle was counting coup. To shoot an enemy from a distance was not as heroic as riding up and actually striking a foe.

Eager to prove themselves in battle, young men joined war parties led by experienced warriors known for their courage, skill, and good luck. War parties raided camps to steal horses—another way of counting coup—or to avenge a relative who had been killed by an enemy. Young men usually became members of one of the warrior societies when they were between thirteen and sixteen years old. Most of the able-bodied men in the band belonged to one of the warrior societies, which included the Kit Fox, or Fox Soldiers; Elk-horn Scrapers,

A Cheyenne Dog Soldier dressed in traditional clothing, including leggings and a breastplate made of hairbone.

now known as the Blue Soldiers; Red Shields, or Bull Soldiers; Bowstring Soldiers; Chief Soldiers; Crazy Dogs; and **Dog Soldiers**, or Dog Men. The most famous were the Dog Soldiers, highly regarded for their bravery and prowess. Besides fighting in battles, the warrior societies maintained order in the band. Because of their honored position, chiefs often consulted the warrior societies on matters of peace.

Hunting Bison

Using lances and arrows, men hunted bison in several ways. Occasionally, a man stalked and killed a single animal. Other times, small hunting parties swept down on a few grazing bison. However, most often, the Cheyenne planned a large hunt in late summer that involved the entire band. At this time, men were not allowed to hunt alone because they might cause the herd to stampede. In a group hunt, everyone in the band—men, women, and children—formed a V and drove the herd over a cliff or into a corral made of stones and brush. Setting a circle of small fires around the herd was another effective method. Afraid to cross the flames and smoke, the bison could then be easily shot with bows and arrows.

After the bison hunt, the women butchered the carcasses strewn over the plains. Everyone shared the meat—giving was very important to the Cheyenne, especially for those who were the ablest hunters and warriors. The liver and other organs that quickly spoiled in the summer heat were cooked and eaten right away. The tongue, hump meat, and ribs were also eaten while fresh. Most of the meat, however, was packed on travois and hauled back to camp, where it would be thinly sliced and hung on poles to dry in the sun. Smoke from fires under the wooden racks kept the flies away and quickened the drying time. Women pounded some of the dried meat, called jerky, and mixed it with berries and fat to make **pemmican**, a food the men could take on long journeys. However, most of the dried meat was stored until the long and lean winter months.

People also made good use of the bison's horns, hide, and bones. Men made tools such as knives, scrapers, and needles from the bones. They also fashioned the bones into smoking pipes and toys. Horns were used to make spoons, cups, and ladles. The women turned the hides into tipi covers, robes, blankets, clothing, and moccasins. Rawhide was made into drums, and the thick neck skin was shaped into effective war shields. Scraped to resemble white parchment, skins were folded to make parfleches for storing belongings. The hooves were made into rattles, and the tail made an excellent flyswatter. Rawhide strips could be woven into sturdy ropes, and sinew was used as sewing thread. For the Cheyenne, a single bison provided many useful objects.

Preparing and Making Food

Along with tanning hides and making tipis, Cheyenne women gathered and prepared food for their families. When they were living in the forests of Minnesota and, later, the Dakotas, they grew corn, beans, and squash. They also gathered fruits, seeds, nuts, berries, and roots. After they moved south and west of the Missouri River, they abandoned farming altogether and primarily hunted bison. They supplemented their diet of bison meat with wild turnips, prickly pear cactus, and corn obtained through trade with other tribes. When the Cheyenne began to trade with settlers, they added coffee, sugar, and flour to their foodstuffs.

RECIPE

BISON BURGER

INGREDIENTS

1 pound (454 grams) ground bison (or buffalo) meat
salt and pepper, to taste
1 tablespoon (15 g) butter or vegetable oil
4 hamburger buns

Divide ground meat into four patties, at least a ½-inch thick.
Fry in skillet with butter or vegetable oil for about six to
eight minutes on each side, or until no longer pink. Lightly
toast the buns, if you wish. Season meat to taste with salt
and pepper and serve on the buns, along with ketchup,
mustard, pickles, onions, or whatever toppings you prefer.

Pemmican was another common and popular food. To make this high-energy food, nuts and wild cherries or plums were crushed and dried in the sun then mixed with pounded meat and some tallow or marrow fat. Women stored pemmican in parfleche bags or buffalo intestines or stomachs. Liquid tallow was poured on top to seal the contents and make the container airtight. In this way, pemmican could be kept for years. Children enjoyed pemmican as a snack, but it was primarily used as food by war parties. It was eaten only when the men did not have time to hunt. In camp, people ate pemmican only when other food was scarce.

Most meats were roasted over a fire or boiled in soups or stews. To boil food, women dug a pit in the ground and lined it with animal skins or a bison stomach. After filling the pit with water, they dropped in heated stones to boil the meat and vegetables.

Clothes and Accessories

Women made their families' clothing from deer or elk hides and later, after they ventured onto the plains, from buffalo skins. They often adorned buckskin with fringes and decorated clothing with dyed porcupine quills. A time-consuming process, the hollow quills were cut into short pieces and carefully sewn onto the garment. When the Cheyenne encountered European traders, they acquired glass beads, which quickly replaced the quills as decoration.

During warm weather, men wore only fringed breechcloths and moccasins made from soft buckskin. As the icy winds of the northern plains bore down upon them, they donned buckskin leggings and shirts and wrapped themselves in bison robes. The leggings were adorned with quills or beads.

A man's clothes reflected his prowess as a warrior and often depicted heroic deeds in his life. Great warriors also wore headdresses of eagle feathers or the horns of bison. War shirts were generally knee-length and decorated with ornate quill and bead designs. They were painted with symbols of dragonflies and thunderbirds or images of the sun, moon, and stars. After their separation in the 1830s, the Northern and Southern Cheyenne became distinguishable partly for the way they dressed. Northern Cheyenne were generally more heavily adorned, while the Southern Cheyenne favored yellow shirts with dark green fringes. Men often attached medicine bags and eagle feathers to their shirts. Sometimes, warriors trimmed their war shirts with the **scalps** of their enemies.

Women wore long, fringed, buckskin dresses, leggings, and moccasins. They often painted their dresses yellow and decorated them with rows of shells, beads, or elk teeth. Leggings and moccasins were also painted yellow and adorned with quillwork. Women also wore boots, reaching almost to their knees, which combined leggings and moccasins. During the winter, women occasionally wore knee-high boots instead of leggings and moccasins.

Since early times, the Cheyenne wore strings of deer or elk teeth around their necks. Their early ancestors also hammered raw copper obtained from deposits near Lake Superior into shimmering bracelets. Brass rings acquired through trade adorned their arms. Once the Europeans arrived, they also traded for German

A Cheyenne woman, circa 1930.

silver, which they made into medallions, or conchas, and other jewelry. Ears were pierced at an early age, from which they hung shell and quill jewelry. Some women hung strings of shell earrings from their waists.

For important rituals, such as the Sun Dance, men carefully painted their bodies with symbols, then placed wreaths of sage on their heads. They wrapped themselves in ankle-length skirts. Members of the Kit Fox Society wore distinctive headdresses and crescent badges. The Dog Soldiers donned long buckskin sashes and feather headdresses. The more prominent warriors also fringed their leggings with the hair of their enemies. In preparation for battle, men painted their faces with bold, fearsome designs of red, blue, yellow, white, and sometimes black.

Resisting Change

The bands of Cheyenne were fiercely dedicated to their traditions and ways of life. When traders and settlers arrived, they tried to preserve and maintain their identity. The Cheyenne were one of the last Native peoples in the United States to adopt European styles of dress. Over time, though, the Western influences and pressure became difficult to resist. More Cheyenne adopted Western lifestyles, beliefs, and customs. Nevertheless, some Cheyenne held on to their ways of life and history, allowing the tribe to continue today.

The Cheyenne believed that all living things were sacred and deserved respect.

CHAPTER FOUR

Nothing lives long.
Only the earth and
the mountains.

—Cheyenne death song

BELIEFS OF THE CHEYENNE

Before traders and settlers came to Cheyenne country, the tribe developed their own beliefs. These ways of thinking influenced every facet of life from birth to death, including hunting, religion, and traditions. The Cheyenne were a proud people, deeply committed to their history and identity as a nation.

Living Things

To the Cheyenne, all living things, including plants and animals, were sacred. Even the most delicate flower was respected, as were the soil and stones. All were warmed by the same sun and considered one with the universe.

The Cheyenne revered plants and animals. Many of their beliefs and rituals were centered on them. Of the birds, they especially respected hawks, eagles, owls, ravens, and magpies. Birds of prey could help warriors in battle, and eagle feathers were especially prized for their powers. Mule deer and elk were honored for their great endurance. If a man dreamed of them, he would be able to share their power. Similarly, skunks, beavers, and otters had spiritual powers, as did the bear, which, the Cheyenne believed, could heal itself. In ancient times, the coyote and wolf were held so sacred that women would not handle their skins. However, of all the animals, the Cheyenne most revered the bison, or buffalo, the animal that provided for so many of their needs. They prayed to the buffalo spirits and to the buffalo skull for the return of the herds.

The Rule of Gods and Spirits

The Cheyenne believed in two principal gods: Heammawihio and Ahktunowihio. Heammawihio, meaning "the Wise One Above," lived in the sky, the place of the dead. Those who passed away went to live there with this spirit. Ahktunowihio, meaning "the Divine Spirit of the Earth," lived beneath the ground. The Cheyenne asked him to give them food, water, and abundant plants.

Great spirits also lived at each of the four directions. As the Cheyenne prayed to these spirits, they raised their smoking pipes to the sky, to the earth, and then to the east, south, west, and north. Hoimaha, a spirit who looked like a man and was entirely white, lived to the north. He brought snow and cold. During the winter, another spirit, the Thunderbird, retreated south, but returned every spring with lightning, thunder, and rain. Powerful spirits also inhabited springs and streams, as well as hills and bluffs. The Cheyenne believed in monsters that lived underwater and ghosts that occasionally frightened people.

The soul was one's shadow or shade. Called *tasoom* (ta-so-OHM), it was believed to be immortal. Tasoom could be the shadow of any living creature, such as a person, horse, or dog, but not the shade cast by rocks or trees. If a man glimpsed his tasoom, it was a sign that he would die very soon.

Sickness, Evil, and Ceremonial Rituals

The Cheyenne had different rituals for warding off or overcoming evil and sickness. Usually, this involved medicine men, who were skilled in such matters, confronting a patient. Elaborately dressed, the medicine men treated both evil and physical illness as one. They might ritually suck the evil out of a patient and spit it on the ground. During healing rituals, they also blew whistles, beat on drums, shook gourd rattles, and offered prayers. These activities were thought to dispel any evil or sickness from a person.

As with all Native American tribes, the Cheyenne had many ceremonies and rituals to celebrate their

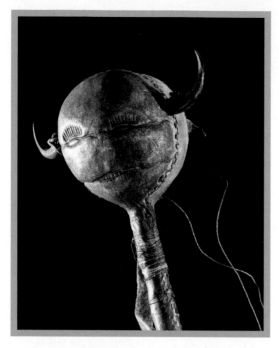

The Cheyenne used rattles in ceremonies and celebrations. This rattle is in the form of a bison head and decorated in rawhide.

history and identity, and to cement their beliefs. The Cheyenne likewise had sacred objects, instruments, and gestures meant to confirm their dedication to such events.

Considered the voice of the Great Spirit, the drum figured prominently in ceremonies. Its round shape symbolized the universe, and its steady beat represented the pulsing heart. It comforted those who were suffering, both in body and in mind.

Before they went into battle or on a hunt, warriors often mutilated themselves to win favor with the spirits. They tore skin off their arms and chest to show their bravery and ability to withstand great pain. Also, these men often fasted for days, hoping it would bring on a vision of a battle's outcome.

Most Sacred Objects

At the heart of Cheyenne worship are several revered objects: the Sacred Arrows (called Maahotse) and the Sacred Medicine Hat (called Esevone), also known as the Sacred Buffalo Hat. The Sacred Arrows are four

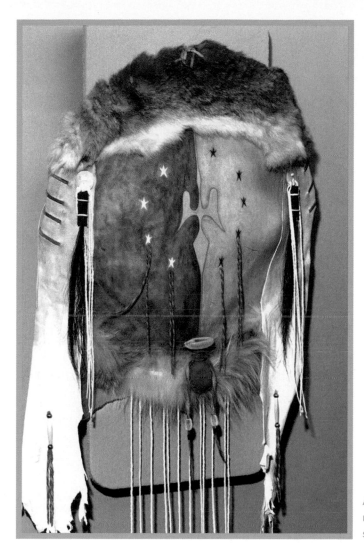

A Cheyenne medicine shield.

arrows belonging to the Cheyenne nation. According to tradition, two are for hunting, when times are tough, and two are for war. Legend says that many years ago, the hero Sweet Medicine came upon the Sacred Arrows near Bear Butte, a peak in the Black Hills. He brought them, wrapped in a bundle, to the people at a time when game was scarce and they were starving. He instructed the people to make arrows just like the sacred ones.

These arrows would allow them to kill many buffalo, and they would no longer be hungry. He also instructed them to keep the arrows he gave them and renew them in a special ceremony each year. According to Sweet Medicine, the arrows had to be kept in a sacred space, wrapped at all times, unless an arrow ceremony was taking place. This ceremony is carried out every year by the Cheyenne tribe today. Since 1877, the Sacred Arrows have been kept by the Southern Cheyenne on the Cheyenne and Arapaho lands in Oklahoma. A special keeper takes care of the arrows.

At the annual renewal ceremony, the Cheyenne reverently open the bundle of Sacred Arrows. Held on the longest day of the year, the Renewal of the Sacred Arrows is the most important Cheyenne ceremony. Each year, the bands set up their tipis in a circle around the Sacred Arrow Lodge. For four days, a medicine man leads the rituals. The arrows' feathers are replaced, and the arrows are tied together in a special bundle. Only the men are allowed to gaze upon the arrows during the renewal. At the end of the four days, the men undergo a purification ritual.

The other venerated object, the Sacred Medicine Hat, was brought to the Cheyenne by the Suhtai tribe. The Suhtai, a tribe that spoke a rougher dialect of the Cheyenne language, officially joined the Cheyenne tribe in the 1830s, although they had lived close to each other and associated with each other for decades. The Sacred Medicine Hat is carefully kept in a bag of buffalo hide, or a medicine bundle with five enemy scalps and a piece of leather fringed with hair known as the Turner. Warriors believe that the Turner has the power to shield them

A Cheyenne member offers the sacred pipe to the ground.

from enemy arrows and bullets. The Sacred Arrows and Sacred Medicine Hat are still honored and protected by the Cheyenne. They are their most sacred objects. The Northern Cheyenne keep their Sacred Medicine Hat in Montana. Like the Sacred Arrows, the Sacred Medicine Hat is housed in a special tipi where a keeper has the honor of caring for it.

Other Traditions

Other major Cheyenne rituals include the Ceremony of the Buffalo and the Sun Dance. The Ceremony of the Buffalo was usually sponsored by a member of the band on behalf of his family or himself and conducted by a medicine man to assure a good hunt. A sweat lodge was built, and a buffalo skull was placed inside on a small earthen mound. People gathered in the sweat lodge to smoke a sacred pipe and make offerings of food to the spirits of the four directions. Over an evening and a day, they sang, prayed, and feasted. Afterward, gifts were made to the individual who had sponsored the ceremony.

Another important ceremony was the Sun Dance. In this annual gathering, the Cheyenne honored the strength of the sun and the renewal of the earth. Having scattered during the winter, all the bands came together as the warm winds of summer again wafted over the grasslands. The Sun Dance Maker and his wife sponsored the event, and a medicine man led it. During the first four days of the ceremony, the Sun Dance Maker and his wife stayed in a special tipi with the medicine man while others in the tribe built the Sun Dance Lodge. This circular structure was centered on a main pole. For the next four days, warriors danced around the pole, singing and praying.

To fulfill their vows and promises, warriors slashed themselves at the end of the dance. Others suspended themselves from the tall pole by attaching rawhide thongs through their chest muscles. Only their toes touched the ground. In great pain and with blood trickling from the wounds, they strained against the rawhide thongs until they tore themselves free. They believed that their sacrifice would ensure that their prayers would be answered. They also thought that the ritual proved their courage and ability to withstand terrible pain. The Cheyenne devoutly practice the Sun Dance each year, but in the modern ritual they rarely submit themselves to the painful rites of the past.

The Cheyenne Stories and Sweet Medicine

With no written language, the Cheyenne passed down their beliefs through stories of war heroes, sacred rites, and the mischief of the character Wihio. Like Coyote in many Native American stories, Wihio was as much a trickster as Sweet Medicine was a hero.

To relate a story was considered a sacred act. According to a member of the Cheyenne tribe named John Stands in Timber, "An old storyteller would smoothe the ground in front of him with his hand and make two marks in it with his right thumb, two marks with his left, and a double mark with both thumbs together … Then he touched the marks on the ground with both hands and rubbed them together and passed them over his head and all over his body. That meant the Creator had made human beings' bodies and their limbs as he had made the earth, and the Creator was witness to what was to be told."

Here is a story about the greatest Cheyenne hero, Sweet Medicine, who helped to save the people, even after he had been treated unjustly:

> After the Cheyenne had received corn and while they were still living in the North, a young man and woman were married. The young woman soon became pregnant but carried the baby in her womb for four years. At last she gave birth to a handsome boy. The parents died before the child was old enough to care for himself, so he was taken in by his grandmother, who lived alone.
>
> People believed that he had supernatural powers, and as soon as the boy was able to walk, he was given a buffalo robe. Sweet

Medicine, or Motzeyoef, as the boy became known, wore his robe with the fur turned to the outside, just like the medicine men. When Sweet Medicine was about ten years old, he wished to take part in the sacred dances of the medicine men. He insisted that his grandmother ask the leader if he could join them. She did so, and the boy was allowed to enter the lodge.

There, Sweet Medicine's body was painted red with black rings around his face. When his turn came to perform, he burned sweetgrass and passed his bowstring through the smoke—east, south, west, and north. Then Sweet Medicine asked the others to assist him. One man tied the bowstring around Sweet Medicine's neck and covered him with the buffalo robe. The boy asked the men to pull the ends of the strings. Although they pulled with all their might, they could not move him. Sweet Medicine then told them to pull harder, and this time his head was cut. They placed the head under the robe with the body. When they lifted the robe, in place of the boy was an old man. When they covered the old man and removed the robe again, they found a pile of bones and a skull. They spread the robe over the bones, and when they lifted it again, they found nothing. Spreading and raising the robe one more time, they found Sweet Medicine.

After the ceremony, the Cheyenne moved their camp in pursuit of the buffalo. The extraordinary boy asked several young men to surround some young buffalo so they could find and kill a two-year-old calf. The boys shot the buffalo with their bows and arrows and began to skin the calf with bone knives. Sweet Medicine told the others to work very carefully, because he wanted the hide complete with head and hooves for a robe.

A chief named Young Wolf approached and demanded the buffalo. Sweet Medicine told the chief that he only wanted the hide and that he would gladly give him the meat, but Young Wolf threw him to the ground. The boy got up and pretended to skin the buffalo, but cut off the leg instead.

While the chief was skinning the buffalo, Sweet Medicine struck him with the buffalo leg and killed him. The other boys ran back to camp and told everyone what had happened. The warriors became angry and decided to pursue Sweet Medicine and kill him. They found the body of the chief, but the boy had already returned to his grandmother's lodge.

The grandmother was cooking in an earthen pot when the warriors arrived at the tipi. Sweet Medicine kicked over the pot, and the food went into the fire. He rose magically in the smoke and disappeared. The warriors found only the old woman sitting alone. Then they saw Sweet Medicine walking away in the distance. Four times they tried to run after him, but each time they were prevented from getting near him.

One morning, a young hunter discovered Sweet Medicine warming himself by a fire in a ravine. Rushing back to camp, he told the warriors and they quickly surrounded the ravine. However, Sweet Medicine had turned into a wolf. Jumping over a high bluff, he ran away, howling at the warriors. Thereafter, the people became afraid of the renegade boy whose strange powers allowed him to elude them so easily.

One day, Sweet Medicine appeared on a nearby hill. Everyone went to see him. He came to the top of the hill again and again, each time in the dress of different warrior societies—Red Shield, Coyote, Dog Soldiers, Hoof Rattle. Finally, he returned with his body painted white and a white owl skin on his forehead. Then he vanished.

Sweet Medicine journeyed alone to the highest mountains. As he approached one of the peaks, a door opened for him. He entered the earth and encountered men representing each of the tribes sitting in a circle. Each held a bundle. The men welcomed Sweet Medicine and invited him to take a seat beneath a fox-skin bundle hanging on the wall. Before he sat down, the head man told the boy he would have to remain with them for four years. Then he would become a Cheyenne prophet.

Sweet Medicine sat down. The men opened the bundle, and inside were four medicine arrows. They instructed the boy in the sacred rituals, and in how to hunt and fight and conduct war. He was to take these instructions back to his people.

During those four years, the Cheyenne experienced a terrible famine. The animals died, and people had only a few plants for food. One day, some children were looking for herbs and mushrooms when Sweet Medicine, now a young man, appeared. He told them, "My poor children, it is I who brought the famine. I was angry because your people drove me away. I have now returned to provide for you so that you will not starve in the future. Gather some buffalo bones, and I will feed you."

The children rushed to bring the bones to him. Sweet Medicine waved his hand over the bones, and they became fresh meat. He fed the children the choicest parts—the fat, marrow, and liver. Then he told them to take the rest of the meat to the people and tell them that he had returned. The children hurried home, but Sweet Medicine reached camp before them and entered his uncle's lodge.

Sweet Medicine was tired, so he lay down to rest in the empty lodge. When his aunt entered to get a pipe, she saw Sweet Medicine covered with a buffalo robe. It was painted red, as were his shirt, leggings, and moccasins. She ran out of the tipi and told the men that someone was there.

Believing it was Sweet Medicine, the men entered the tipi. Everyone cried over the young prophet, overjoyed at his return. Sweet Medicine showed the people his fox-skin bundle and instructed them to set up a large tipi in the center of the camp. He gathered all the medicine men in the tipi and shared the ceremonies and songs as he had been instructed. Frightened by a loud noise, the Cheyenne went to Sweet Medicine. Calmly, he told them, "Go to sleep, for the buffalo have returned to you."

The next morning, the land was covered with buffalo, and the people had an abundance of food, because of the power of Sweet Medicine and the Sacred Arrows.

To the Cheyenne, Sweet Medicine had great influence over the formation of the tribe, and continues to hold a significant place in Cheyenne history. He was the one who brought the Cheyenne the Sacred Arrows and instructed how to care for and renew them. He also is attributed with setting up the Cheyenne's war societies and by instructing them how to arrange their

Chief Charles Little Coyote attends a Medicine Lodge Peace Treaty parade held in 1997.

government. Many in the Cheyenne tribe refer to Sweet Medicine as a savior.

The Cheyenne developed their culture, filled with unique and sometimes harrowing celebrations, over many years. Today, their history is one of the most well preserved and well known of the Great Plains tribes. However, their culture only has remained due to the many efforts of the Cheyenne people. If it were not for them, their culture may have died following struggles with the European and American settlers in the nineteenth and twentieth centuries.

In the 1800s, US settlers wanted more land and moved west to get it.

*All we ask is to be
allowed to live, and to
live in peace.*

—Dull Knife

OVERCOMING HARDSHIPS

P rior to 1848, the Cheyenne had encountered Europeans as traders and explorers. Some settlers had also journeyed to the area, but it was not until after the United States acquired more land following the Mexican-American War in 1848 that an influx of settlers arrived. These people were spurred by the concept of **manifest destiny**, a belief that it was God's right that the American people would span across both coasts of the United States. With the arrival of settlers, the Cheyenne's way of life began to change.

This painting illustrates the overkilling of bison in the 1850s.

Losing the Bison

One of the first and most significant changes to take place on Cheyenne territory was the population of the bison. As settlers drove their **wagon trains** across expansive grasslands, they were quickly confronted by the large beasts. These animals could be used for meat, food, clothing, and sport. Before long, the bison population began to decrease, either from overhunting or from being frightened away by the settlers' wagons. In greater numbers, settlers were killing or taking bison not to use for their survival but for fun. Hunters killed thousands of bison for their hides and left the meat to rot in the sun. Others saw the value in trading bison and rounded up the wild animals to sell and slaughter

The People and Culture of the Cheyenne

as they chose. The herds quickly disappeared until the bison was nearly extinct.

The Cheyenne, along with other Native tribes, grew angry with settlers for encroaching on their land and killing the bison. Bull Bear, a chief of the Dog Soldiers, described the Cheyenne relationship with the bison: "We love them just as the white man does his money. Just as it makes a white man feel to have his money carried away, so it makes us feel to see others killing and stealing our buffaloes, which are our cattle given to us by the Great Spirit above to provide us meat to eat and means to get things to wear." They tried to protect the animals, but in the end, the bison population struggled to survive. Originally, an estimate of sixty million bison roamed the United States, from the Great Plains to the South. By 1884, only around 325 wild bison remained in the United States, according to the US Fish and Wildlife Service.

Soldiers and Settlers

Another issue that led to conflict throughout the second half of the nineteenth century was difficulties between the Cheyenne and US soldiers. The Cheyenne were not the only tribes struggling against these forces, however. Throughout the western United States, Native American tribes encountered troops and sought to conquer them and preserve their land and identity. In the end, most often their efforts led to hardship and heartache.

Along the Platte River on the northern plains, the United States military took over Fort Laramie in 1849. It would be important to Cheyenne history in years to follow. In 1851, eleven tribes assembled at

Fort Laramie in present-day Wyoming in the largest gathering of Native people in history. They were there to discuss preserving their lands and protecting them against settlers, who often would travel through their territory. In response to settlers' presence, some Native groups would confront them, often violently, and prevent settlers from passing safely through Native lands. Some settlers, in return, would attack and kill Native tribe members. Fort Laramie had been set up in hopes to limit the amount of attacks between groups. Nevertheless, these problems continued, so this meeting between the two sides occurred. Between eight and twelve thousand members of the Cheyenne, Sioux, Assiniboin, Crow, Shoshone, and other tribes entered into a treaty that allowed wagon trains headed to Oregon and California to cross their lands without confrontation from Native groups. The United States agreed to station troops on the Great Plains to protect Native people from attacks by settlers. However, the number of settlers increased dramatically over the next five years, and the frequent clashes quickly escalated into a bloody war with the United States Army.

From 1857 to 1879 the Cheyenne fought an ongoing war for their very survival as soldiers swept down on their camps and slaughtered women and children. The bloodiest of these attacks became known as the Sand Creek **Massacre**. In 1864, the great chief Black Kettle, along with groups of Cheyenne and Arapaho, was camped on Sand Creek in the present-day state of Colorado. They were on the edge of what was then **reservation** land. They had been waiting for a delegate of peace, as promised to them in a meeting with US

This hide painting recounts the Sand Creek Massacre in 1864.

Army leaders in October 1864. Chief Black Kettle had wanted peace, and the negotiations met in October seemed to assure that. He had been quoted as saying in September to Colonel John Chivington, a Union officer: "I want you to give all the chiefs of the soldiers here to understand that we are for peace, and that we have made peace, that we may not be mistaken by them for enemies." At the peace meeting, Black Kettle had been told to raise the US flag to denote his people's cooperation and peaceful status until the delegation could arrive. They did so, and waited. By November 29, 1864, they had still no news. However, that morning a horrible attack took place. Seven hundred soldiers under the command of Chivington, a man who wanted to remove all Native people from the West, led a surprise attack on the camp at daybreak while the people slept.

George Bent, who was part Cheyenne and lived with the band, described the slaughter: "Black Kettle had a large American flag up on a long lodge pole as a signal to the troop that the camp was friendly. Part of the people were rushing about the camp in great fear. All the time Black Kettle kept calling out not to be frightened, that the camp was under protection and there was no danger. Then suddenly the troops opened fire."

One hundred and five Cheyenne and Arapaho women and children and twenty-eight men were slaughtered in the Sand Creek Massacre. The survivors fled but were quickly pursued by Chivington and his troops. After a time, the soldiers returned to the scene of the attack. They mutilated the dead and took scalps or other body parts as souvenirs.

Bent described the camp after the ruthless attack: "Everyone was crying, even the warriors, and the women and children were screaming and wailing. Nearly everyone present had lost some relatives or friends, and many of them in their grief were gashing themselves with their knives until the blood flowed in streams."

In Denver, the soldiers displayed their "trophies" to curious spectators and many people considered the soldiers heroes. However, others, especially along the East Coast, were horrified by what they heard. They were disgusted by Chivington and his actions. As a result, Chivington had to give up his position in the Union Army.

The Sand Creek Massacre embittered the Cheyenne and forever changed their view of the United States. Black Kettle declared, "I once thought that I was the only man that persevered to be the friend of the white man, but since they have come and cleaned out our lodges, horses, and everything else, it is hard for me to believe white men any more."

Despite the US government's attempt to assuage the Cheyenne's pain by providing compensation for them in the Treaty of the Little Arkansas River in 1865, the damage done was permanent. The Sand Creek Massacre is one of the worst attacks on Native people in their history and is forever emblazoned into the memories of the Cheyenne people. In 2014, the grounds of the attack became the Sand Creek Massacre National Historic site, commemorating the event and bringing it permanently to the forefront of the history of the American West.

Railroads were built on the Cheyenne homeland throughout the 1850s and 1860s.

Railroads

In addition to confrontations with US troops and settlers, another threat to Native land was the railway. The advent of these railway lines enabled huge stretches of land to be connected and people to be transported from one end of the country to the other. However, it also meant Native territory was diminished and ignored to make way for railroad track and towns surrounding the rail lines. While a transcontinental railway system was not completed until 1869, Native groups, including the Cheyenne, felt the struggle to preserve their old ways of life with the many laborers and settlers such a technology brought to the region. In retaliation, some members of the Cheyenne tore up railway tracks and caused problems for the workers there.

Moving to Reservations

In 1867, under the provisions of the Medicine Lodge Treaty, the Cheyenne and Arapaho were assigned to a reservation. The reservation was located north of the Washita River in Indian Territory, now present-day Oklahoma. Although placed on the same reservation, the Cheyenne and Arapaho insisted on having separate tribal organizations. With no interest in trying to farm the poor soil and receiving only meager rations, which were often withheld, the Cheyenne suffered terribly in confinement. They felt like prisoners in this new land.

The Indian Wars

Back in Colorado, the remaining bands of Cheyenne tried to preserve their identity and resist efforts to move them south. In some instances, war societies such as the Dog Soldiers took it upon themselves to drive settlers and soldiers from the land, often resulting to violence and murder. In response, US soldiers retaliated.

The Cheyenne joined in the Indian War that swept over the Great Plains from the summer through the

The People and Culture of the Cheyenne

early winter of 1868. On November 27, soldiers from the US Seventh Cavalry under the command of Colonel George Armstrong Custer attacked Black Kettle and his band along the Washita River. Many Cheyenne, including Black Kettle, were killed in this engagement. Many of their horses were slaughtered, and their camp was destroyed. The next year saw more bloodshed and loss. In 1869, many members of the Dog Soldiers, including their leader Tall Bull, were killed at the Battle of Summit Springs. Following the confrontations in 1868 and 1869, the Cheyenne became even more bitter enemies of the US government. They strongly resisted all efforts to remove them from their homeland.

The Battles of 1876

On June 17, 1876, Sioux and Cheyenne warriors engaged General George Crook's cavalry and infantry at Rosebud in Montana. It led to the Native American victory eight days later against George Armstrong Custer on the Little Bighorn River. The Battle at Rosebud occurred after an order had been made for all Sioux to reside on reservation land set aside for them. The government determined that any member of the tribe not to do so would be deemed hostile and could be pursued, forcibly moved to the reservation, or killed. Members of Sioux chief Sitting Bull's tribe would not be persuaded. Sitting Bull knew a battle was imminent. To get more soldiers, he called to the Creator, asking for help and to see a vision of the battle's outcome. In return, he promised to hold a two-day Sun Dance ceremony in thanks. Warriors from the Lakota, Cheyenne, and Arapaho tribes joined him.

After performing the Sun Dance ceremony, Sitting Bull saw the battle's outcome and had it drawn on a rock: It was an image of upside down soldiers. Inspired by this, members of the Lakota tribe, led by warrior Crazy Horse, ventured to General Crook's camp and attacked, eventually forcing Crook's retreat. Just over a week later, the Battle of Little Bighorn raged.

General Custer had been an opponent of the Cheyenne and other Native American tribes for many years. He had led campaigns against the Southern Cheyenne and had been involved in their defeat at Washita River in 1868. An accomplished Civil War soldier, Custer had hopes to defeat the Native forces in 1876. He and his men ventured to a Native village and split into three groups, hoping to ensure that no Native person escaped.

That day, the Northern Cheyenne united with Sioux warriors and played a prominent role in the destruction of Custer and his forces. Numbering more than two thousand warriors, several bands, including the Cheyenne, were camped with Crazy Horse and Sitting Bull. Encountering twice as many warriors as he had expected, Custer attacked anyway. Two Moon, a Cheyenne chief who led his warriors against Custer, described the battle: "Then the Sioux rode up the ridge on all sides, riding very fast. The Cheyennes went up the left way. Then the shooting was quick, quick. Pop—pop—pop very fast. Some of the soldiers were down on their knees, some standing. Officers all in front. The smoke was like a great cloud, and everywhere the Sioux went, the dust rose like smoke. We circled all around them—swirling like water round a stone. We shoot, we

The People and Culture of the Cheyenne

ride fast, we shoot again. Soldiers drop, and horses fall on them."

Custer's foolish attack resulted in his death and the loss of his entire force of 225 men. "One man all alone ran far down toward the river, then round up over the hill. I thought he was going to escape, but a Sioux fired and hit him in the head. He was the last man," Two Moon recalled.

News of the defeat reached the East Coast on July 5, 1876, spoiling celebrations of the United States centennial. The Battle of the Little Bighorn was the greatest of Native American victories. However, Two Moon recalled, "We had no dance that night. We were sorrowful." In fact, the conflict provoked sweeping retaliation from the United States that soon ended the Plains tribes' way of life. After the battle, Cheyenne, Sioux, and other Plains people were relentlessly hunted down. Those who were not massacred were forced onto reservations in Indian Territory.

Struggles to Survive

In the spring of 1877, the Northern Cheyenne who had lodged with Crazy Horse during the winter finally surrendered to General Nelson Miles at Fort Keogh in Montana. The Northern Cheyenne were sent to the reservation in Oklahoma, but they could not adjust to the hot climate. Adding to their misery, many people contracted malaria, and half the band died. In August 1878, two chiefs, Little Wolf and Dull Knife (also known as Morning Star), asked Indian **agent** John Miles to allow them to move back to their northern ranges. Sick and hungry, the Cheyenne longed to return to their homeland.

After declaring that they were going home and did not wish to fight, Dull Knife and Little Wolf led 353 Northern Cheyenne from the reservation on September 9, 1878. Dull Knife later recalled, "We bowed to the will of the Great Father and went far into the south where he told us to go. There we found a Cheyenne cannot live. Sickness came among us that made mourning in every lodge. Then the treaty promises were broken, and our rations were short. Those not worn by diseases were wasted by hunger. To stay there meant that all of us would die." They were heading for their home country on the Powder River in Wyoming and Montana about 1,500 miles (2,414 km) away. But they did not get far before two companies of cavalry caught up with them.

The Cheyenne refused promises of fair treatment and **skirmished** with the soldiers. "Our petitions to the Great Father were unheeded. We thought it better to die fighting to regain our old homes than to perish of sickness," Dull Knife explained. Enduring freezing cold and starvation, they bravely fought pursuing soldiers in a heroic effort to reach home. As they continued toward the northwest, they warded off several more attacks and crossed the Arkansas and South Platte Rivers. The band eluded ten thousand soldiers and three thousand civilians for six weeks in a 1,500-mile (2,414 km) journey. At White Clay Creek in Nebraska, they split into two groups. Although they had fought off or eluded the soldiers, the one hundred fifty people in Dull Knife's group were exhausted and hungry. He led them to the

The People and Culture of the Cheyenne

Red Cloud Agency, where they planned to surrender. Little Wolf took about the same number to the Nebraska Sand Hills, where they spent the winter. The following March, Little Wolf led his band to the mouth of the Powder River, where they engaged Lieutenant W. P. Clark, who was himself guided by Cheyenne and Sioux scouts. Clark convinced Little Wolf to surrender to General Miles at Fort Keogh.

In Nebraska, Dull Knife found the Red Cloud Agency abandoned, so he and his band traveled to Fort Robinson. They lived at the fort for two months, awaiting orders. Finally, they learned that they were to be sent back to Indian Territory. Refusing to be moved against his will, Dull Knife declared, "I am here on my own ground, and I will never go back. You may kill me here, but you cannot make me go back." Captain Wessells, the commanding officer, then imprisoned the Cheyenne in an unheated barracks with no food or water. On January 9, 1879, Little Shield, a Dog Soldier Society chief, led a daring breakout. Fifty people died fighting for their lives in the snow. Twenty more died of their wounds and exposure to the bitter cold. Fewer than a hundred now, the band was driven back to Fort Robinson.

Meanwhile, thirty-one other warriors who had escaped Fort Robinson hid out at Hat Creek Bluffs, where they were trapped. All but three men were shot dead. Even when they had exhausted their ammunition, the warriors staunchly refused to give up. Using their guns as clubs, the remaining three charged the soldiers and were gunned down. Later, the bones of the dead men were given to the Army Medical Museum for scientific research. The remains were not returned to the Cheyenne until October 8, 1993, for reburial under the Native American Graves Protection and Repatriation Act of 1990.

Dull Knife, his wife, and his son were among a small number of Northern Cheyenne who managed to escape Fort Robinson and head north. They walked for eighteen nights, eating bark and their own moccasins. When they arrived at the Pine Ridge Agency in present-day South Dakota, Bill Rowland, an interpreter, sheltered them. Along with other Northern Cheyenne who had managed to reach the North, they were then moved to a reservation on the Tongue River, in southeastern Montana near the Wyoming state line. In 1883, the last of the Northern Cheyenne in Indian Territory were also allowed to settle there. An executive order on November 26, 1884, formally set aside this tract of land for the Northern Cheyenne.

The bison that had once blackened the Great Plains were nearly gone, however, and both the Northern and Southern Cheyenne became dependent on the government for food, clothing, and shelter. Attempts were made to bring cattle to the Oklahoma and Montana reservations and encourage the people to become ranchers, but government officials opposed the plan. The Cheyenne made the best of their restrictions. "Yes, it is pleasant to be situated where I can sleep soundly at night without fear," Wooden Leg said of reservation life. However, the Cheyenne warrior, who had encamped at Little Big Horn during Custer's last stand, added, "I wish I could live again through some of the past days of real freedom."

This painting depicts the battle that has become known as Custer's Last Stand.

Under the Dawes Act, the Southern Cheyenne were assigned individual **allotments** of land in Oklahoma in 1887. Their remaining tribal lands were then opened up for American settlers on April 19, 1892. With their land taken away, the Cheyenne became scattered and their culture threatened. Fred Last Bull predicted what would happen when Americans, driven by their own technology, took away Cheyenne territory: "They will be a powerful people, strong, tough. They will fly up into the sky, they will dig under the earth, they will drain the earth and kill it. All over the earth they will kill the trees and the grass, they will put their own grass and their own hay, but the earth will be dead—all the old trees and grass and animals."

Today, the bands of Cheyenne still exist: the Cheyenne-Arapaho Tribes still live in Oklahoma, and the Northern Cheyenne are based in Montana. They have redefined their communities and started their own schools, and they have their own government. They are federally recognized as sovereign nations.

Preserving the Language

Cheyenne belongs to the great Algonquian language family of North America, which includes Ojibwe, Mohican, Delaware, Shawnee, and Blackfoot, among others. The Cheyenne language is taught in reservation schools and at home. While many Native American people, including the Cheyenne, know English, today there are more Native Cheyenne speakers, and the language is gaining popularity. The Cheyenne Arapaho Language Department also has Cheyenne language lessons on their YouTube channel, making it easy to learn at a time that is convenient for students.

The following examples are based on the *English-Cheyenne Student Dictionary*, produced by the Language Research Department of the Northern Cheyenne in Lame Deer, Montana. Here is the Cheyenne alphabet, and examples of the pronunciation:

a	as in father
e	as in pit or pet
o	as in go

The consonants are generally pronounced as in English. Additional sounds are *s* as in *she*, known as the "esh" and *x* as in the German "A*ch*tung!"

? is the glottal stop, a catch in the throat, as in the space between "uh oh!"

´ is a stress mark to emphasize a vowel

- is a separation mark between syllables

Also, be sure to fully pronounce every letter and syllable.

Everyday Words

maahe	arrow
náhkohe	bear
ve?keso	bird
hetané-ka?eskone	boy
hotóva?a	buffalo (male)
méhe	buffalo (female)
ka?eskóne	child
mahaemenotse	corn (kernel)
vaotseva	deer
oeskeso	dog
mené?kesono	doll
ho?e	earth
netse	eagle
voazáa?e	bald eagle

nóma?he	fish
máhtame	food
séstotó?e-se?e	forest
oónaha?e	frog
hé?e-ka?eskone	girl
na-venovo	home (my)
mo?éhe-no?ha	horse
ho?e	land
hetane	man
taa?é-ese?he	moon
ho?honáae-vose	mountain
heskóvestse	porcupine
tóhtoo?e	prairie
ónone-vóneske	prairie dog
heskóvestsee?e	quill, porcupine
ó?he?e	river
vano?estse	sagebrush
hésta?se	snow
ése?he	sun
ma?eno	turtle
mahpe	water
haa?háese	wind
h?eé	woman

Body Parts

ma-?ahtse	arm or hand
ma-tonese	belly
ma-tseeseeo?o	chest
ma-htsé?oo?o	elbow
ma?éxa	eye
mo?esko	finger
me?ko	head
ma-nestane	knee
mahtse	mouth
ma-htse?otse	neck
ma?évo	nose
ma-htatamoo?o	shoulder

The Cheyenne tribes have endured much in relatively recent history. Through their struggles, they have maintained their presence and their history as Native people. Their determination to continue their tribal traditions, customs, and beliefs testifies to their resilience in the face of difficulty.

Today, the Cheyenne
continue to celebrate
the traditions of their
ancestors through song
and ceremony.

CHAPTER SIX

Socieities who do not care for their young people and old people are decadent, decaying societies.

—Suzan Shown Harjo, Cheyenne member

THE NATION'S PRESENCE NOW

Today, the once-unified Cheyenne Nation exists as two main bands, the Northern Cheyenne in Lame Deer, Montana, and the Southern Cheyenne in Concho, Oklahoma. This division of Northern and Southern groups was made official with the signing of the First Treaty of Fort Laramie in 1851; however, the groups had been separated since as early as 1832. Both

This young boy rides his horse next to a mural on the Northern Cheyenne reservation in Lame Deer, Montana.

tribes continue the ways of their ancestors and celebrate a common language. In addition to living in different areas of the United States, the Cheyenne have different traditional ways of dress and celebrations throughout the year. Their shared history remains integral to their identities as Cheyenne members today. For many years, the tribes have struggled for recognition from the federal government to gain **sovereignty** for their people. Today, conditions on the reservations have improved, and the groups have been offered certain levels of autonomy; however, struggles remain.

According to the state of Montana's official website, mt.gov, ten bands comprise the Cheyenne Nation. These bands are spread out "all over the Great Plains, from southern Colorado to the Black Hills of South Dakota." Many direct and indirect descendants form

The People and Culture of the Cheyenne

the Cheyenne Nation. In 2015, an estimated twenty thousand people were directly descended from Cheyenne tribe members.

The Northern Cheyenne Tribe Today

Today, the Northern Cheyenne live closest to their western ancestral lands. The Northern Cheyenne Reservation covers over 440,000 acres (178,061 hectares) and is bounded on the east by the Tongue River, on the west by the Crow Reservation in Big Horn County, and on the north by Rosebud County. The total Northern Cheyenne tribal enrollment is nearly 10,900, about 4,939 of whom live on the Montana reservation. About one in five families makes its home in rural areas along the streams and rivers. The rest live in the small towns of Lame Deer, Busby, and Ashland, on or near the reservation. The Northern Cheyenne Reservation is 99 percent tribally owned. It makes many of its own laws, has its own school district, and offers its own tribally-run activities.

The reservation also encompasses landmarks that echo the Cheyenne past, including a historical buffalo jump in the rugged backcountry, the burial places of great chiefs, and Custer's last camp before the Battle of the Little Bighorn. The battle site borders the reservation. Each year, the tribe hosts several powwows, including Labor Day, Fourth of July, and Memorial Day powwows. They participate in annual Native American tribal activities, such as the All Nations Indian Relay Championships.

For many years, the Cheyenne struggled to live on the reservation. The discovery of coal on the Northern Cheyenne reservation in the 1960s promised to bring

A Cheyenne dancer wearing ceremonial dress.

desperately needed revenue to the struggling tribe, but many tribal leaders feared that only outside investors would profit, leaving residents still impoverished. They were also deeply concerned about the possible environmental damage in strip-mining their lands. Others disagreed, believing the mines would not only provide jobs but allow the reservation to establish educational and health programs and improve living conditions. However, those who opposed strip-mining prevailed in the 1970s, thereby saving their beloved land. When grants were awarded for drilling operations in the 1980s, no gas or oil was discovered, and the tribe was left with financial difficulties.

Partly in response to the discovery of coal, in 1975 the Dull Knife Memorial College was established. Named after the Northern Cheyenne great leader, the college was renamed Chief Dull Knife College in 2001 to better honor the great man. It was initially started to train students in the ways of the mining industry,

The People and Culture of the Cheyenne

This is the scene of the Battle of the Washita, during which Chief Black Kettle was killed. Today, this grassland is named the Black Kettle National Grassland in his honor.

but over time, it has expanded its curriculum offerings. Today it awards several associate's degrees, online degrees, and training certifications. Nearby, the St. Labre School District in Ashland, Montana, offers primary and secondary education for Native and non-Native students. As of 2015, the district teaches 750 students.

Since the 1970s, the Northern Cheyenne have also managed a small bison herd as a joint venture with T. R. Hughes, a private philanthropist from Seward, Nebraska. The tribe provided pasture and tended the herd in exchange for half the calves born each season. The Cheyenne have increased the herd from 50 bison in 2005 to 170 bison in 2015.

To learn more about the Northern Cheyenne, you can visit their website: www.cheyennenation.com.

The Southern Cheyenne Tribe Today

Today, the Southern Cheyenne share a tribal office with their old friends and allies, the Southern Arapaho, in Concho, Oklahoma. The two tribes have about 80,000 acres (32,374 ha) held in trust near the Washita Battle Ground Historic Site in the Black Kettle National Grassland. Gas and oil have been found on this land near the Canadian River, west of Oklahoma City. These resources have helped alleviate the poverty of the Southern Cheyenne. Today, these industries have bolstered finances in the area and on tribal land. Together, the total population of Cheyenne and Arapaho in Concho equals 4,876, although the total tribal enrollment for both groups totals 12,200.

The Cheyenne and Arapaho community offers activities year-round for people to explore their cultures. Some unique experiences include learning about horse culture from a Cheyenne or Arapaho member, learning Native songs and dances, watching annual powwows, and attending language immersion camps. One of the most successful language preservation actions taken by the tribes is the Cheyenne and Arapaho Language Training Program. This program instructs members of the Native community in mastering the Cheyenne or Arapaho language, in the hope that they will teach their tongue to others and increase the number of Native speakers.

Like the Northern Cheyenne, the Southern Cheyenne and Arapaho tribes have their own bison herd. According to the community's website, it is the

A young man dances the fancy dance at the Cheyenne Celebration in 2007.

The Nation's Presence Now

largest tribal bison herd in Oklahoma. As of 2015 there are "currently 260 head of [bison] on 3,000 acres [1,214 ha] of native grasslands."

The tribe for many years struggled to adjust to a Southern lifestyle. Throughout the 1960s and 1970s, conditions were tough. However, the groups worked together and voiced their concerns. They came back from a difficult situation. In 2011, the tribes drafted a plan to help their community develop and ensure its future. In it, they suggested ways of making their tribe more accessible to visitors by remodeling signs and informational areas, creating more walk-friendly areas in the nearby towns, and encouraging others to get involved with community life through learning the language and participating in community events. Likewise, they outlined their desire to continue using the land for activities such as farming and coal mining, and discussed how the community would confront issues concerning the environment, recycling, and a growing elderly population.

As every Native American tribe struggles to maintain their identity and embrace the technological world of the twenty-first century, the Southern Cheyenne and Arapaho tribes have taken steps to ensure they link the two worlds together. The community has aired its own TV channel, CATV47, since 2012. It is Oklahoma's first entirely tribally-run and -owned TV network. In September 2014, the Cheyenne and Arapaho tribes teamed with the Oklahoma Educational Television Authority to create a Native American TV show called *Native Oklahoma*. Each episode of the program focuses on a different Oklahoma tribe and is produced by the tribe in question. It is a unique experience that brings the history of the tribe alive on screen.

To learn more about the tribe, visit their website: www.c-a-tribes.org.

Learning from the Past

Both the Northern and Southern Cheyenne have fought for better education and better-paying jobs. Both branches live in two worlds—that of their ancestors and the modern culture of twenty-first century America. The Cheyenne want to succeed economically, yet they also wish to continue the traditions and ceremonies of the past. While many have become teachers, doctors, ranchers, and business executives, they still strive to preserve their shared heritage. They believe that their honored traditions, notably the Sacred Buffalo Hat and Sacred Medicine Arrows, will guide them into a prosperous future.

The two Cheyenne groups have distinct characteristics but are connected by shared values and history. Both the Cheyenne groups remember their past and pass their knowledge on through the generations. By doing so, they ensure their continued presence in the world and the continuance of the Cheyenne Nation as a whole.

Chief Black Kettle, his men, and several agents gather for a photograph in September 1864. Two months later, many of these men would die at the Sand Creek Massacre.

CHAPTER SEVEN

Do not judge your neighbor until you walk two moons in his moccasins.

—Cheyenne saying

FACES OF THE CHEYENNE

Throughout its history, the Cheyenne Nation has seen many heroes and noteworthy individuals. Some have lived long lives full of happiness, while others have endured many challenging and life-changing obstacles. These are the names and histories of a few of the most prominent figures in Cheyenne history.

Black Kettle (circa 1807–1868), Southern Cheyenne, peace chief, became a warrior in his youth. He fought the Ute, Delaware, and other Cheyenne enemies. However, by the 1860s, he came to advocate peace with settlers and soldiers. During the spring of 1864, Colonel John Chivington led a military campaign that resulted in the slaughter of many Cheyenne and Arapaho, including women and children. Even though his good friend Lean Bear was killed in the campaign, Black Kettle refused to go to war. On November 29, Chivington attacked Black Kettle's camp at Sand Creek, ignoring Black Kettle's flag of truce. Black Kettle managed to escape, but more than one hundred people were killed, over half of them women and children. Despite the massacre, Black Kettle still advocated peace with the whites. In 1867, he signed a treaty at Medicine Lodge in which the Southern Cheyenne, Southern Arapaho, Comanche, and Kiowa received tribal lands in Oklahoma. Yet settlers violated the treaty, and some warriors raided in retaliation. This led to a war with American soldiers, when Lieutenant Colonel George Armstrong Custer's forces approached Black Kettle's camp on the Washita River on November 27, 1868. Black Kettle rode out in hopes of preventing the attack, but the soldiers fired upon the chief and his wife, killing them. The soldiers then swept through the camp, killing around one hundred people, mostly women and children.

Ben Nighthorse Campbell (1933–), Northern Cheyenne political leader and former US senator, was born in Auburn, California, to an Apache-Pueblo-Cheyenne father and Portuguese-American mother. Enlisting in the air force in 1951, he served in the Korean War (1950–1953) where he learned a type of martial arts called judo. After earning a college degree in physical education and fine arts, he continued to

Ben Nighthorse Campbell in 2013.

study judo at the highly regarded Meiji University in Tokyo, Japan, where he became a sixth-degree black belt. He won a gold medal at the 1963 Pan-American Games, but the following year, he lost in the Olympics due to a knee injury.

He subsequently became a teacher, horse breeder and trainer, and a talented designer and maker of jewelry. In 1980, he was enrolled as a member of the Northern Cheyenne tribe and was later inducted into the Council of 44 Chiefs. In 1982, he was elected to the Colorado house of representatives and in 1986, he was elected to the US House of Representatives, where he served three terms. He was elected to the US Senate in 1992 and shocked voters by changing his party affiliation from Democrat to Republican. He is the first Native American to chair the Senate Committee on Indian Affairs, remaining an eloquent spokesman for the rights and interests of all Native Americans. He resigned from his role in the Senate in 2005, and today he is most known for creating beautiful jewelry.

Dull Knife (Tahmelapashme, Wohehiv, Morning Star) (ca. 1810–1883), a Northern Cheyenne war chief, fought in the Cheyenne-Arapaho War in Colorado in 1864–1865. He was one of the signers of the Second Fort Laramie Treaty of 1868. He was active in the Sioux Wars on the northern plains, joining Sitting Bull and Crazy Horse in the war for the Black Hills of 1876–1877.

On November 25, 1876, US soldiers led by Colonel Ranald S. Mackenzie attacked Dull Knife's camp on the Red Fork of the Powder River in what became known as the Battle of Dull Knife. The following May, Dull Knife, Little Wolf, and their bands surrendered at Fort Robinson in Nebraska. They expected to be sent to the Sioux Reservation in the Black Hills, but instead they joined the Southern Cheyenne and Arapaho in Indian Territory in present-day Oklahoma.

Life was difficult on the barren land, with few supplies and outbreaks of malaria. On September 9, 1878, Dull Knife and Little Wolf led nearly three hundred people, including women and children, northward to their homeland on the Tongue River in Wyoming and Montana. The band eluded soldiers and civilians for six weeks in a 1,500-mile (805 km) journey, but Dull Knife led the sick and hungry to Red Cloud's reservation, while Little Wolf continued with the rest to Montana. However, Dull Knife's group was eventually captured and held at Fort Robinson. On a bitterly cold night, they broke out when they learned they were to be sent back to Oklahoma. Pursuing troops killed nearly half of the members, including Dull Knife's daughter. Only Dull Knife, his wife, son, daughter-in-law, grandchild, and another person escaped. They journeyed to Red Cloud's reservation at Pine Ridge and were hidden by friends until caught by the pursuing army.

Little Wolf and his band hid out for the winter but were also found and encouraged to surrender on the Little Missouri River in Montana. The survivors were finally allowed to remain in the north. In 1884, the Northern Cheyenne were granted the Tongue River Reservation in Montana. Dull Knife had died the year before. He was buried on a high butte near the Rosebud River.

Suzan Shown Harjo (1945–), a Southern Cheyenne activist, was born in El Reno, Oklahoma. Since 1974, she has worked vigorously to reshape federal policies regarding Native Americans, assuring the passage of more than three hundred legislative initiatives. Her

Suzan Shown Harjo attends an exhibition at the Smithsonian Institute's National Museum of American Indians in 2014.

efforts include the Indian Health Care Improvement Act, Indian Self-Determination and Education Assistance Act, American Indian Religious Freedom Act, and fifteen bills to restore lands to tribes throughout the western United States.

During the 1970s, she also served as a special assistant in the Office of the Secretary of the Interior. While in this position, she was the coordinator and principal author of the Report to Congress on American Indian Religious Freedom. From 1984 to 1989, she served as executive director of the National Congress of American Indians (NCAI) and co-chair of the NCAI Legislation and Litigation Committee.

A member of the Cheyenne and Arapaho tribes, she is an advocate for women's rights as well as a journalist and an accomplished poet.

Lean Bear (Starved Bear) (died 1864), a Northern Cheyenne peace chief, was involved in an incident at the Fort Atkinson Council. He noticed a ring on the hand of an officer's wife and grabbed her arm for a better look. She cried out, and her husband attacked Lean Bear with a whip. The Cheyenne threatened war, and Thomas Fitzpatrick, the Indian agent who had called the meeting, gave a blanket to Lean Bear in an act of goodwill.

In later years, Lean Bear, along with his good friend Black Kettle, worked for peace. In 1863, he joined a peace delegation to Washington, DC, that included Ten Bears of the Comanche and Lone Wolf of the Kiowa. The chiefs met with President Abraham Lincoln to discuss a long-term treaty. The following year, while on a buffalo hunt, Lean Bear noticed a group of soldiers under the command of Colonel John Chivington. When the troops formed for battle, Lean Bear and Star, another Cheyenne, rode forward to state their peaceful intentions. Lean Bear was wearing a peace medal and carrying papers in his hand, signed by Lincoln, stating that he was a friend of the whites. However, the soldiers fired on the two Cheyenne, who fell to the ground. The soldiers advanced and shot them again. The death of Lean Bear and the Sand Creek Massacre soon triggered more conflict. Lean Bear's brother, Bull Bear, and other Cheyenne Dog Soldiers intensified their attacks in the Cheyenne-Arapaho War of 1864–1865 and other warfare on the southern plains.

Little Robe (1828–1886), Southern Cheyenne, was a renowned warrior in battles with the Ute, Pawnee, and other enemies of the Cheyenne. After he distinguished himself in a fight with the Pawnees on the Beaver River in Kansas in 1852, he was given the great honor of carrying the Pipe of Mourning to the camps. Around 1863, he became a chief.

After the Sand Creek Massacre of 1864, Little Robe took part in raids on settlers in the Cheyenne-Arapaho War. Yet he soon came to believe that warfare was hopeless, and he began to advocate peace. Along with Black Kettle and George Bent, he tried to encourage the Dog Soldiers to sign the Medicine Lodge Treaty of 1867. When Black Kettle died in 1868 at the Battle of Washita, Little Robe became the principal chief among the Cheyenne who advocated peace. Subsequently, he surrendered to General Philip H. Sheridan at Fort Cobb in Indian Territory. In 1873, he visited Washington, DC, with Stone Calf, White Horse, White Shield, and other leaders to meet with President Ulysses S. Grant. When the Comanche, led by Quanah Parker, and the Kiowa, led by Lone Wolf, fought in the Red River War of 1874–1875, Little Robe continued to seek peace.

Later in life, he lived on the North Canadian River in Indian Territory. Although he wished to get along with settlers, he sought to sustain traditional Cheyenne culture and refused to send children from his band to white schools. With Stone Calf and White Calf, he also worked to keep ranchers' cattle herds off reservation land.

Little Wolf (Ohkom Kakit) (ca. 1820–1904), a Northern Cheyenne leader of the Bowstring Soldiers, achieved fame as a warrior against the Comanche and Kiowa. In later years, he fought with other Northern Cheyenne, Sioux, and Arapaho warriors in many battles against US soldiers on the northern plains. From 1866 to 1868, in Red Cloud's War, or the War for the Bozeman Trail, he fought with the great Sioux leaders Crazy Horse and Gall.

In 1868, he was one of the signers of the Fort Laramie Treaty. However, in July of that same year, after warriors had driven the soldiers from the Powder River region, Little Wolf and his band joined in the occupation of Fort Phil Kearney, Wyoming. A month later, they abandoned and burned the fort. Fighting under the command of Sitting Bull, Little Wolf was one of the most vigorous leaders in the War for the Black Hills in 1876–1877. During the Battle of Dull Knife, he was shot seven times but managed to get away. He evaded capture for several months, but he eventually surrendered and was sent to Indian Territory in present-day Oklahoma.

Little Wolf joined Dull Knife in the flight of the Northern Cheyenne back to their homeland in September 1878. North of the Platte River, they split into two groups. Dull Knife finally surrendered in October, but Little Wolf and his group eluded pursuing soldiers until March of the following year. He was finally convinced to report to Fort Keogh. Little Wolf and a few warriors became army scouts for General Nelson A. Miles and were allowed to remain in the Tongue River country. However, Little Wolf killed a Cheyenne named Starving Elk in a dispute. Because he had killed another Cheyenne, Little Wolf lost his position as chief. He went into voluntary exile along the Rosebud River, where he lived until his death.

Roman Nose

Southern Cheyenne chief Roman Nose (*right*) and his wife (*left*).

(Woquini, Waquini, Wokini) (1830–1868), a Southern Cheyenne leader in the war of the southern Plains, became a noted warrior in battles with settlers and soldiers. After the massacre at Sand Creek, Roman Nose fought in the Battle of Platte Bridge in July 1865 with Sioux warriors led by Red Cloud. He told General Winfield Scott Hancock, "Cheyenne warriors are not afraid, but have you never heard of Sand Creek? Your soldiers look just like those who butchered the women and children there." He also took part in the War for the Bozeman Trail. In 1866, he journeyed south to fight with the well-known Dog Soldiers, which included Bull Bear, Tall Bull, and White Horse. The warriors raided along the Kansas frontier, attacking wagon trains and railroad work crews and eluding the Seventh Cavalry under Colonel George Armstrong Custer. Roman Nose warned them, "If the palefaces come farther into our land, there will be scalps of your brethren in the wigwams of the Cheyenne."

Pursued by soldiers during the summer of 1868, Roman Nose and his fellow warriors attacked a company of troops under the command of Major George Forsyth on the Arikaree branch of the Republican River in Colorado. Believing that his "medicine," or good fortune, had been broken, Roman Nose did not lead the first charge. Fully expecting to die in battle, he spent the morning in preparation. That afternoon, during a charge, he was shot in the spine. He died that night in the Cheyenne camp. Shaken by the loss of Roman Nose, the warriors fought halfheartedly until September 25, then retreated. To the Cheyenne, the engagement has since been known as the Fight When Roman Nose Was Killed.

Stone Calf (died 1885), a Southern Cheyenne, was a famous warrior during his youth, but along with Black Kettle and Little Robe he later encouraged peaceful relations with settlers and soldiers. In 1868, he met with Indian agent Edward Wynkoop and General Philip H. Sheridan. Two years later, in 1870, he met with Quaker agents who were reviewing President Ulysses S. Grant's peace policy in the Indian Territory. Along with Little Robe, he served as a spokesman for the Cheyenne, returning two years later for further talks. Stone Calf tried to keep his warriors from taking part in the Red River War of 1874–1875 with the Comanche and Kiowa. He was unsuccessful, and his son was killed in the Battle of Adobe Walls in June 1874.

Living near the army's post, Stone Calf became an important leader on the reservation. He opposed a grass-lease program that permitted ranchers to graze their cattle on Cheyenne land. He argued that there was not enough grass for tribal horses and that the cowboys mistreated the Cheyenne. His vigorous efforts helped to end the leasing program.

Tall Bull (Hotoakhihoosis, Hotuaeka'ash, Otoah-hastis) (ca. 1815–1869) was a prominent Southern Cheyenne leader of the Dog Soldiers along with Bull Bear and White Horse during the 1850s and 1860s. After the Sand Creek Massacre, he and the other Dog Soldiers intensified their attacks on settlers. Following the Civil War, Tall Bull met with General Winfield Scott Hancock at Fort Larned in Kansas in 1867. However, their peace talks broke down. That summer, George Armstrong Custer and the Seventh Cavalry pursued the Dog Soldiers, as well as Sioux and Arapaho warriors, but failed to catch them.

Government officials initiated two treaties: the Medicine Lodge Treaty of 1867 and Fort Laramie Treaty of 1868. Tall Bull was present at the Medicine Lodge Treaty, as were other Cheyenne chiefs. However, in 1868, Tall Bull and his warriors violated the terms of the treaty by attacking the Kaw (Kansas) tribe. As a result, government officials refused to distribute guns and ammunition for hunting to the Southern Cheyenne. The Dog Soldiers responded by assaulting settlers on the Sabine and Solomon Rivers in Kansas. Soldiers under the command of General Philip H. Sheridan launched the Sheridan Campaign. In response, Tall Bull and the other Dog Soldiers took part in several battles, including the attack in which Roman Nose was killed, and the Battle of Washita, in which Black Kettle died.

The Sheridan Campaign continued through the spring and summer of 1869. Little Robe and other peace chiefs finally brought their followers to the Cheyenne and Arapaho Reservation. However, Tall Bull led his warriors north to the area of the Republican River, where they raided the Kansas frontier. Major Eugene A. Carr organized an expedition to stop them and attacked Tall Bull's camp. After a counterattack, Tall Bull and his warriors escaped. However, the troops finally caught up with the Cheyenne at Summit Springs in Colorado. In what came to be known as the Battle of Summit Springs, fifty-two warriors were killed and seventeen women and children were captured. Tall Bull was among the dead. The survivors scattered northward to Sioux territory. This battle marked the end of the Dog Soldiers' prominence on the Great Plains.

The men and women who make up the Cheyenne tribe today remember these historical figures and celebrate the people still with the tribe. They have seen the tribe and the land change over the years and have enacted change for the tribe's benefit in more recent years. Without these figures in society, the Cheyenne tribe may be quite different today.

CHRONOLOGY

1680 French explorer René-Robert Cavelier, Sieur de La Salle, encounters a camp of Cheyenne on the Illinois River.

late 1600s The Cheyenne begin to migrate to the Great Plains from the area of the Great Lakes.

circa 1760 The Cheyenne acquire horses and learn to become expert riders. Adopting a nomadic way of life, they become one of the dominant tribes of the Great Plains.

1803 The United States purchases the Louisiana Territory from France, a vast area that included Cheyenne home country and led to US westward expansion. In the following years, trading posts are established throughout the West.

1804 The Cheyenne meet American explorers Meriwether Lewis and William Clark on their trek to the Pacific coast.

circa 1832 The tribe splits into the Northern and Southern Cheyenne.

1837–1870 At least four smallpox epidemics ravage the tribes of the Great Plains.

1849 The United States government purchases Fort Laramie from the American Fur Company and posts troops there.

1851 The Cheyenne are one of the eleven tribes to sign the Fort Laramie Treaty, permitting settlers to pass across their territories. Wagon trains of settlers travel over what becomes known as the Bozeman Trail.

1862 The Homestead Act leads to a flood of settlers onto tribal lands, including the Great Plains. The Cheyenne resist this invasion.

1864 Colonel John Chivington leads a troop of volunteers and soldiers in an attack against Black Kettle's camp, slaughtering Cheyenne and Arapaho men, women, and children in what became known as the Sand Creek Massacre.

1876 The Cheyenne unite with the Sioux in destroying George Armstrong Custer and his forces at the Battle of the Little Bighorn.

1877 Over one thousand Northern Cheyenne join the Southern Cheyenne in present-day Oklahoma.

1884 The Northern Cheyenne Reservation is established in southeastern Montana.

1887 The General Allotment Act, or Dawes Act, reduces tribal land by giving 160 acres (65 ha) to each family and 80 acres (32 ha) to individuals with so-called "surplus lands" opened for settlement.

1880s The US government prohibits the Sun Dance of the plains tribes.

1900 Fewer than one thousand buffalo remain on the Great Plains.

about 1900 The tribal lands of the Southern Cheyenne are divided into allotments to be owned by individual members.

1924 The United States recognizes all Native Americans born within the states and territories as citizens.

1934 The Indian Reorganization Act recognizes tribal governments and provides financial assistance.

1960 Coal is discovered on land owned by the Northern Cheyenne, leading to controversy over possible mining.

1975 Dull Knife Memorial College is established.

1992 Ben Nighthorse Campbell is elected to the US Senate.

2001 Dull Knife Memorial College is renamed to Chief Dull Knife College.

2012 The Cheyenne Arapaho TV network CATV47 begins airing.

2014 CATV47 airs the show *Native Oklahoma* in partnership with the Oklahoma Educational Television Authority and other tribes living in Oklahoma.

2014 The Southern Cheyenne participate in the 42nd annual Red Moon Powwow in May; the Cheyenne and Arapaho remember 150 years since the Sand Creek Massacre; Sand Creek Massacre National Historic Site opens.

GLOSSARY

agent A US government employee responsible for undertaking official business with a Native tribe.

allotment The US government policy of dividing tribal lands into small tracts to be owned by individuals. Also, one of the tracts.

Bering Strait The body of water that separates Russia and Alaska. During the last Ice Age, a land bridge across the strait allowed for migration from one continent to the other.

count coup To touch an enemy in battle to prove one's bravery.

cradleboard A wooden board used to carry a baby.

Dog Soldiers One of the warrior societies of the Cheyenne, considered to be the best fighters.

Great Plains A vast area of prairie stretching across North America from Texas to Canada.

manifest destiny The concept that it was the right of the American people to settle the country from coast to coast.

massacre The deliberate and ruthless slaughter of a large number of people.

moccasin A soft leather shoe often decorated with brightly colored beads.

nomadic Moving periodically from one place to another.

pemmican Pounded dry meat mixed with fat and berries used as "energy food" by warriors on long journeys.

quillwork Decorative embroidery patterns created with the quills of porcupines or birds.

reservation A tract of land set aside as a home for Native Americans.

scalp A lock of hair and skin from the head of an enemy.

skirmish To fight a minor battle, usually as part of an ongoing war.

sovereignty The right and ability of a people to govern themselves and their nation.

Sun Dance An important Cheyenne ceremony held every summer.

sustenance Food or drink that nourishes the body.

sweat lodge A dome-shaped hut covered with buffalo skins in which purifications and other sacred ceremonies are held.

tipi A cone-shaped house made of poles covered with animal skins.

travois A sled made of two poles lashed together and pulled by a dog or horse.

treaty A signed, legal agreement between two nations.

wagon trains Groups of settlers that traveled together in several wagons.

The People and Culture of the Cheyenne

BIBLIOGRAPHY

Agnew, Jeremy. *Life of a Soldier on the Western Frontier.* Missoula, MT: Mountain Press Publishing, 2008.

Bausch, Robert. *Far As the Eye Can See.* New York: Bloomsbury, 2014.

Blackhawk, Ned. *Violence Over the Land: Indians and Empires in the Early American West.* Cambridge, MA: Harvard University Press, 2008.

Broome, Jeff. *Cheyenne War: Indian Raids on the Roads to Denver 1864-1869.* Sheridan, CO: Aberdeen Books, 2013.

———. *Dog Soldier Justice: The Ordeal of Susanna Alerdice in the Kansas Indian War.* Lincoln, NE: University of Nebraska Press: 2009.

Donovan, James. *A Terrible Glory: Custer and the Little Bighorn—The Last Great Battle of the American West.* New York: Back Bay Books, 2008.

Enss, Chris, and Howard Kazanjian. *Mochi's War: The Tragedy of Sand Creek.* New York: TwoDot Press, 2015.

Greene, Jerome A. *Washita: The US Army and the Southern Cheyennes, 1867–1869*. Campaigns and Commanders. Norman, OK: University of Oklahoma Press, 2008.

Halaas, David F., and Andrew E. Masich. *Halfbreed: The Remarkable True Story of George Bent—Caught Between the Worlds of the Indian and the White Man*. Cambridge, MA: Da Capo Press, 2004.

Hatch, Thom. *Black Kettle: The Cheyenne Chief Who Sought Peace but Found War*. Hoboken, NJ: Wiley, 2004.

Hyde, Anne F. *Empires, Nations, and Families: A New History of the North American West, 1800–1860*. New York: HarperCollins, 2011.

Kelman, Ari. *A Misplaced Massacre: Struggling Over the Memory of Sand Creek*. Cambridge, MA: Harvard University Press, 2013.

Rinella, Steven. *American Buffalo: In Search of a Lost Icon*. New York: Spiegel & Grau, 2009.

Wallis, Michael. *The Wild West: 365 Days*. New York: Abrams, 2011.

The People and Culture of the Cheyenne

FURTHER INFORMATION

Want to know more about the Cheyenne? Check out these websites, videos, and organizations.

Websites

Dog Soldiers

www.manataka.org/page164.html

This article explains who the Dog Soldiers were and their significance in Cheyenne history.

George Armstrong Custer

www.history.com/topics/george-armstrong-custer

This website describes the history behind one of the most infamous men in US history.

Smithsonian: Horrific Sand Creek Massacre Will Not Be Forgotten

www.smithsonianmag.com/history/horrific-sand-creek-massacre-will-be-forgotten-no-more-180953403

This review of the Sand Creek Massacre highlights why it is important to remember this event.

Visit Montana: Northern Cheyenne Reservation

www.visitmt.com/listings/general/indian-nation/northern-cheyenne-indian-reservation.html

This website gives an overview of the Northern Cheyenne Reservation.

Videos

Rocky Mountain PBS: Sand Creek Massacre

www.youtube.com/h?v=dDnPT1qYa64&list=PL54418F6FB571A532&index=20

This video discusses the details that led to the Sand Creek Massacre, the event itself, and the aftermath of the attack.

Two Southern Cheyenne Songs

www.youtube.com/watch?v=upBsqNZYTsw&list=PLUOQ2BZqxW3dqc-juhu_2qwFNb1blr3FB

This video allows you to listen to two Southern Cheyenne songs performed by members of the tribe.

Organizations

Cheyenne-Arapaho of Oklahoma

100 Red Moon Circle
Concho, OK 73022
(405) 422-8267
www.c-a-tribes.org

Chief Dull Knife College

1 College Drive
Lame Deer, MT 59043
(406) 477-6215
www.cdkc.edu

Northern Cheyenne

PO Box 128
Lame Deer, MT 59043
(406) 477-6284
www.cheyennenation.com

Sand Creek National Historic Site

910 Wansted
PO Box 249
Eads, CO 81036
(719) 438-5916
www.sandcreeksite.com

St. Labre Indian School

Ashland, MT 59004
(406) 784-4500
www.stlabre.org

INDEX

Page numbers in **boldface** are illustrations. Entries in **boldface** are glossary terms.

The People and Culture of the Cheyenne

The People and Culture of the Cheyenne

ABOUT THE AUTHORS

Cassie M. Lawton is a freelance editor and writer living and working in New York City.

Raymond Bial has published more than eighty books— most of them photography books—during his career. His photo-essays for children include *Corn Belt Harvest, Amish Home, Frontier Home, Shaker Home, The Underground Railroad, Portrait of a Farm Family, With Needle and Thread: A Book About Quilts, Mist Over the Mountains: Appalachia and Its People, Cajun Home,* and *Where Lincoln Walked.*

As with his other work, Bial's deep feeling for his subjects is evident in both the text and illustrations. He travels to tribal cultural centers, photographing homes, artifacts, and surroundings and learning firsthand about the national lifeways of these peoples.

The emeritus director of a small college library in the Midwest, he lives with his wife and three children in Urbana, Illinois.